SIDE by SIDES

PRESTWICK HOUSE, INC.

MUCH ADO
ABOUT
NOTHING

WILLIAM SHAKESPEARE

Shakespeare's text

on the left;

modern rendering

on the right.

PRESTWICK
H O U S E
INCORPORATED

P.O. Box 658 • Clayton, DE 19938
Tel: 1.800.932.4593
Web site: www.prestwickhouse.com

ISBN 978-1-58049-515-8

Table of Contents

DRAMATIS PERSONAE

DON PEDRO, Prince of Arragon
DON JOHN, his bastard brother
CLAUDIO, a young lord of Florence
BENEDICK, a young lord of Padua
LEONATO, Governor of Messina
ANTONIO, an old man, his brother
BALTHASAR, attendant on Don Pedro
BORACHIO, follower of Don John
CONRADE, follower of Don John
FRIAR FRANCIS
DOGBERRY, a Constable
VERGES, a Headborough
A Sexton
A Boy

HERO, daughter to Leonato
BEATRICE, niece to Leonato
MARGARET, gentlewoman attending to Hero
URSULA, gentlewoman attending to Hero

Act I

Scene 1
Before Leonato's House

[Enter Leonato, Hero, Beatrice, and a messenger.]

LEONATO: I learn in this letter that Don Pedro of Arragon comes this night to Messina.

MESSENGER: He is very near by this. He was not three leagues off when I left him.

5 LEONATO: How many gentlemen have you lost in this action?

MESSENGER: But few of any sort, and none of name.

LEONATO: A victory is twice itself when the achiever brings home full numbers. I find here that Don Pedro hath bestowed much honour on a young Florentine called Claudio.

10 MESSENGER: Much deserved on his part, and equally remembered by Don Pedro. He hath borne himself beyond the promise of his age, doing in the figure of a lamb the feats of a lion. He hath indeed better bettered expectation than you must expect of me to tell you how.

15 LEONATO: He hath an uncle here in Messina who will be very much glad of it.

Act I

Scene 1
Before Leonato's House

[Enter Leonato, Hero, Beatrice, and a messenger.]

LEONATO: *This letter informs me that Don Pedro, the prince of Arragon, is coming to Messina tonight.*

MESSENGER: *He is indeed very close. He was less than ten miles away when I left him.*

LEONATO: *How many gentlemen have you lost in this battle?*

MESSENGER: *Very few, and none from an important family.*

LEONATO: *Victory is doubly sweet when the leader brings full numbers home. I see here that Don Pedro has bestowed much honor on a young Florentine, Claudio.*

MESSENGER: *They were richly deserved and Don Pedro rewarded him accordingly. Claudio has carried himself like a veteran, doing the feats of a lion while looking like a lamb. Indeed, my poor words can scarcely begin to tell of his accomplishments.*

LEONATO: *He has an uncle here in Messina who will be very happy to hear it.*

MESSENGER: I have already delivered him letters, and there appears much joy in him; even so much that joy could not show itself modest enough without a badge of bitterness.

20 LEONATO: Did he break out into tears?

MESSENGER: In great measure.

LEONATO: A kind overflow of kindness. There are no faces truer than those that are so washed. How much better is it to weep at joy than to joy at weeping!

25 BEATRICE: I pray you, is Signior Mountanto returned from the wars or no?

MESSENGER: I know none of that name, lady. There was none such in the army of any sort.

LEONATO: What is he that you ask for, niece?

30 HERO: My cousin means Signior Benedick of Padua.

MESSENGER: O, he's returned, and as pleasant as ever he was.

BEATRICE: He set up his bills here in Messina and challenged Cupid at the flight; and my uncle's fool, reading the challenge, sub-scribed for Cupid and challenged him at the birdbolt. I pray
35 you, how many hath he killed and eaten in these wars? But how many hath he killed? For, indeed I promised to eat all of his killing.

LEONATO: Faith, niece, you tax Signior Benedick too much; but he'll be meet with you, I doubt it not.

40 MESSENGER: He hath done good service, lady, in these wars.

MESSENGER: *I have already given him some letters and he appears very happy. In fact, he was so happy that he couldn't contain himself without showing some bitter sign.*

LEONATO: *Did he break into tears?*

MESSENGER: *In great quantity.*

LEONATO: *A natural expression of kindness. There are no more honest faces than those cleaned this way. It is so much better to cry for happiness than to be happy at sad events.*

BEATRICE: *Excuse me, my lord, but has Signior Sword-Whacker returned from the battle?*

MESSENGER: *I don't know anyone by that name, miss. There wasn't anyone like that in the army.*

LEONATO: *Niece, who is it you ask about?*

HERO: *My cousin means Signior Benedick of Padua.*

MESSENGER: *Oh, he's returned, and he's as well as he ever was.*

BEATRICE: *He once posted an archery challenge in Messina to Cupid and my uncle's jester read the challenge, stood in for Cupid, and dueled him with harmless weapons. But, my lord, how many men has he killed and eaten in this battle? How many has he killed? Indeed, I promised to eat everything he ever killed.*

LEONATO: *Well, niece, you attack Signior Benedick too severely; he'll get even with you, I'm sure.*

MESSENGER: *He has done good work, miss, in these wars.*

7

BEATRICE: You had musty victual, and he hath holp to eat it. He is a very valiant trencherman; he hath an excellent stomach.

MESSENGER: And a good soldier too, lady.

BEATRICE: And a good soldier to a lady; but what is he to a lord?

45 MESSENGER: A lord to a lord, a man to a man; stuffed with all honourable virtues.

BEATRICE: It is so indeed. He is no less than a stuffed man; but for the stuffing—well, we are all mortal.

LEONATO: You must not, my lord, mistake my niece. There is a kind of merry war betwixt Signior Benedick and her. They never 50 meet but there's a skirmish of wit between them.

BEATRICE: Alas! He gets nothing by that. In our last conflict four of his five wits went halting off, and now is the whole man governed with one; so that if he have wit enough to keep himself warm, let him bear it for a difference between himself and 55 his horse; for it is all the wealth that he hath left to be known a reasonable creature. Who is his companion now? He hath every month a new sworn brother.

MESSENGER: Is't possible?

BEATRICE: Very easily possible. He wears his faith but as the fashion 60 of his hat; it ever changes with the next block.

MESSENGER: I see, lady, the gentleman is not in your books.

BEATRICE: No, and if he were, I would burn my study. But I pray you, who is his companion? Is there no young squarer now that will make a voyage with him to the devil?

8

BEATRICE: You had stale food, and he had helped you eat it. He is a very valiant eater; he has an exceptional stomach.

MESSENGER: And he's a good soldier, too, lady.

BEATRICE: And a good soldier to a lady; but what is he to a lord?

MESSENGER: A lord to a lord, a man to a man; filled with all noble virtues.

BEATRICE: Indeed, it is so. He is like a stuffed scarecrow; except for the stuffing—well, we are all mortal.

LEONATO: Excuse my niece, my lord. There's a sort of "merry war" between Benedick and her. Whenever they meet, there's a war of words between them.

BEATRICE: Well, he doesn't understand that. In our last battle four of his five mental faculties went limping away, and now the entire man is run by only one. If he's now smart enough to keep himself warm, let him praise it as a difference between himself and his horse since that is the only way we will know him to be a reasonable creature. Who is his new companion? He has a new friend every month.

MESSENGER: Is it possible?

BEATRICE: Very possible, indeed. He shows his allegiance like a fashionable hat; it changes with the style.

MESSENGER: I see, miss, that Benedick is not in your book of friends.

BEATRICE: No, and if he were, I would burn my study. But I ask you, my lord, who is his new found friend? Isn't there some young quarreller who will go to the devil with him?

65   MESSENGER: He is most in the company of the right noble Claudio.

BEATRICE: O Lord, he will hang upon him like a disease! He is sooner
        caught than the pestilence, and the taker runs presently mad.
        God help the noble Claudio! If he have caught the Benedick, it
        will cost him a thousand pound ere he be cured.

70   MESSENGER: I will hold friends with you, lady.

BEATRICE: Do, good friend.

LEONATO: You will never run mad, niece.

BEATRICE: No, not till a hot January.

MESSENGER: Don Pedro is approached.

[Enter Don Pedro, Claudio, Benedick, Balthasar, and Don John the
Bastard.]

75   DON PEDRO: Good Signior Leonato, are you come to meet your
        trouble? The fashion of the world is to avoid cost, and you
        encounter it.

LEONATO: Never came trouble to my house in the likeness of your
        Grace; for trouble being gone, comfort should remain; but
80   when you depart from me, sorrow abides and happiness takes
        his leave.

DON PEDRO: You embrace your charge too willingly. I think this is
        your daughter.

LEONATO: Her mother hath many times told me so.

85   BENEDICK: Were you in doubt, my lord, that you asked her?

10

MESSENGER: *He is mostly in the company of the noble Claudio.*

BEATRICE: *God! He will hang on Claudio like a disease! It's easier to catch him than to catch the plague; and the victim will be driven crazy. God help poor Claudio! If he has caught "the Benedick," it will cost him dearly before he finds a cure.*

MESSENGER: *I will be sure to remain friends with you, miss.*

BEATRICE: *Do, good friend.*

LEONATO: *You won't ever catch "the Benedick," niece.*

BEATRICE: *No, not until there's a hot January.*

MESSENGER: *Don Pedro is coming.*

[Enter Don Pedro, Claudio, Benedick, Balthasar, and Don John the Bastard.]

DON PEDRO: *Well, Signior Leonato, have you come to greet your troubles? The fashion of the world is to avoid trouble; and yet, you go out of your way to meet us.*

LEONATO: *Lord, you could never be a trouble to my household. When troubles leaves, happiness is evident; but when you leave, happiness goes too, and only sorrow remains.*

DON PEDRO: *You welcome your problem very warmly [turning to Hero] and I believe this is your daughter.*

LEONATO: *Her mother has told me that many times.*

BENEDICK: *Since you asked her, my lord, did you doubt that fact?*

11

LEONATO: Signior Benedick, no; for then were you a child.

DON PEDRO: You have it full, Benedick. We may guess by this
what you are, being a man. Truly, the lady fathers herself. Be
happy, lady; for you are like an honourable father.

90 BENEDICK: If Signior Leonato be her father, she would not have his
head on her shoulders for all Messina, as like him as she is.

BEATRICE: I wonder that you will still be talking, Signior Benedick;
Nobody marks you.

BENEDICK: What, my dear Lady Disdain! are you yet living?

95 BEATRICE: Is it possible Disdain should die while she hath such
meet food to feed it as Signior Benedick? Courtesy itself must
convert to disdain if you come in her presence.

BENEDICK: Then is courtesy a turncoat. But it is certain I am loved
of all ladies, only you excepted; and I would I could find in
100 my heart that I had not a hard heart, for truly I love none.

BEATRICE: A dear happiness to women! They would else have been
troubled with a pernicious suitor. I thank God and my cold
blood, I am of your humour for that. I had rather hear my dog
bark at a crow than a man swear he loves me.

105 BENEDICK: God keep your ladyship still in that mind! So some
gentleman or other shall scape a predestinate scratched face.

BEATRICE: Scratching could not make it worse an 'twere such a face
as yours were.

BENEDICK: Well, you are a rare parrot-teacher.

LEONATO: No, Signior Benedick, for you were only a child then.

DON PEDRO: You've got your answer, Benedick. By this, we know what kind of man you are. Indeed, the lady resembles her father. Be happy, miss, for you are like your honorable father.

BENEDICK: As much as she resembles her father, she wouldn't want his head on her body for all the riches in this town.

BEATRICE: I'm amazed that you're still babbling, Signior Benedick. No one is paying attention to you.

BENEDICK: What, my dear Lady Disdain! Are you still alive?

BEATRICE: Could it be possible for Disdain to die when she has such suitable food to feed upon as you? Pleasantness changes to abuse when you appear.

BENEDICK: Then courtesy is a traitor. Certainly, I'm loved by all women, except you; and I wish I could change my cold heart, for I really don't love anyone.

BEATRICE: A great happiness to women, or else they would be troubled by a malicious suitor. I thank God that I agree with you about that. I would rather hear my dog bark at a crow than hear a man swear he loves me.

BENEDICK: I hope God keeps that thought in your mind so some man escapes from getting his face scratched.

BEATRICE: Scratching couldn't make it worse if it were a face like yours.

BENEDICK: Why, you are a rare parrot talker.

110 BEATRICE: A bird of my tongue is better than a beast of yours.

BENEDICK: I would my horse had the speed of your tongue, and so good a continuer. But keep your way, a God's name! I have done.

BEATRICE: You always end with a jade's trick. I know you of old.

115 DON PEDRO: That is the sum of all, Leonato. Signior Claudio and Signior Benedick, my dear friend Leonato hath invited you all. I tell him we shall stay here at the least a month, and he heartly prays some occasion may detain us longer. I dare swear he is no hypocrite, but prays from his heart.

120 LEONATO: If you swear, my lord, you shall not be forsworn. [To Don John] Let me bid you welcome, my lord. Being reconciled to the prince your brother, I owe you all duty.

DON JOHN: I thank you. I am not of many words, but I thank you.

LEONATO: Please it your Grace lead on?

125 DON PEDRO: Your hand, Leonato. We will go together.

[Exeunt all but Benedick and Claudio.]

CLAUDIO: Benedick, didst thou note the daughter of Signior Leonato?

BENEDICK: I noted her not, but I looked on her.

CLAUDIO: Is she not a modest young lady?

BEATRICE: *A bird that speaks like me is better than an animal that sounds like you.*

BENEDICK: *I wish my horse had the quickness of your tongue, and could run as long as you talk. Well, have it your way, I'm done.*

BEATRICE: *You always end when I'm just getting started. I know your tricks from the past.*

DON PEDRO: *Well, Leonato that is the end of that. [turning to Claudio and Benedick] Claudio, Benedick, my good friend Leonato has invited us to stay at least a month with him. I swear that he is welcoming us from his heart.*

LEONATO: *If you swear upon that point, my lord, you will not be proved a liar. [To Don John] Let me welcome you also, my lord. Since you are reconciled with your brother, I owe like allegiance to you.*

DON JOHN: *Thank you. I'm not very talkative, but I thank you.*

LEONATO: *Would your highness lead us into the house?*

DON PEDRO: *Give me your hand, Leonato. We will go together.*

[All exit except Benedick and Claudio.]

CLAUDIO: *Benedick, did you notice Signior Leonato's daughter?*

BENEDICK: *I didn't notice her, but I saw her.*

CLAUDIO: *Is she not the prettiest young lady?*

130   BENEDICK: Do you question me, as an honest man should do, for my simple true judgment? or would you have me speak after my custom, as being a professed tyrant to their sex?

CLAUDIO: No. I pray thee speak in sober judgment.

BENEDICK: Why, i' faith, methinks she's too low for a high praise,
135   too brown for a fair praise, and too little for a great praise. Only this commendation I can afford her, that were she other than she is, she were unhandsome, and being no other but as she is, I do not like her.

CLAUDIO: Thou thinkest I am in sport. I pray thee tell me truly how
140   thou likest her.

BENEDICK: Would you buy her, that you enquire after her?

CLAUDIO: Can the world buy such a jewel?

BENEDICK: Yea, and a case to put it into. But speak you this with a sad brow? or do you play the flouting Jack, to tell us Cupid
145   is a good hare-finder and Vulcan a rare carpenter? Come, in what key shall a man take you to go in the song?

CLAUDIO: In mine eye she is the sweetest lady that ever I looked on.

BENEDICK: I can see yet without spectacles, and I see no such matter. There's her cousin, an she were not possessed with a fury,
150   exceeds her as much in beauty as the first of May doth the last of December. But I hope you have no intent to turn husband, have you?

CLAUDIO: I would scarce trust myself, though I had sworn the contrary, if Hero would be my wife.

BENEDICK: *Do you want an honest answer? Or do you want my usual answer since you know I disparage all of that sex?*

CLAUDIO: *No, please give me your honest appraisal.*

BENEDICK: *Well, I think she's too low for a high praise, too dark for a fair praise, and too small for a huge praise. I can only say this; that if she were different than she is, she could be homely, but being as she is, I do not like her.*

CLAUDIO: *You think I'm joking. Really, please tell me how you like her.*

BENEDICK: *Why? Do you want to know in order to purchase her?*

CLAUDIO: *Can anyone buy such a treasure?*

BENEDICK: *Yes, and clothes to wrap around it. But do you speak this seriously, or are you teasing? Are you telling me that blind Cupid has great eyesight and the blacksmith Vulcan is really a carpenter? In what key should a man follow your tune?*

CLAUDIO: *In my eyes, she is the prettiest lady I've ever seen.*

BENEDICK: *I can see without glasses, and I don't see anything of the kind. Now, there's her cousin who, if she didn't have such a temper, surpasses her in beauty as spring does winter. But I hope you're not thinking of getting married?*

CLAUDIO: *Despite my past statements, I would if Hero would be my wife.*

155 BENEDICK: Is't come to this? In faith, hath not the world one man
but he will wear his cap with suspicion? Shall I never see a
bachelor of threescore again? Go to, i' faith! An thou wilt
needs thrust thy neck into a yoke, wear the print of it and
sigh away Sundays. Look; Don Pedro is returned to seek you.

[Re-enter Don Pedro.]

160 DON PEDRO: What secret hath held you here, that you followed not
to Leonato's?

BENEDICK: I would your Grace would constrain me to tell.

DON PEDRO: I charge thee on thy allegiance.

BENEDICK: You hear, Count Claudio. I can be secret as a dumb man,
165 I would have you think so; but, on my allegiance—mark you
this—on my allegiance! he is in love. With who? Now that is
your Grace's part. Mark how short his answer is: With Hero,
Leonato's short daughter.

CLAUDIO: If this were so, so were it uttered.

170 BENEDICK: Like the old tale, my lord: 'it is not so, nor 'twas not so;
but indeed, God forbid it should be so!'

CLAUDIO: If my passion change not shortly, God forbid it should be
otherwise.

DON PEDRO: Amen, if you love her; for the lady is very well worthy.

175 CLAUDIO: You speak this to fetch me in, my lord.

DON PEDRO: By my troth, I speak my thought.

BENEDICK: Has it come to this? Does every man want to worry about an unfaithful wife? Will I never see a 60 year old bachelor again? Come on! Will you wear the yoke of marriage, bear its weight and pine away on Sundays? Look! Here comes Don Pedro to see you.

[Re-enter Don Pedro.]

DON PEDRO: What secret has kept you from following us to Leonato's?

BENEDICK: I wish your lordship would force me to tell you.

DON PEDRO: I bid you tell me by your oath of loyalty.

BENEDICK: You hear, Claudio. I can keep a secret as well as a mute. Really. But by my loyalty, notice, by my loyalty—Claudio is in love! With whom? Your grace can take this part. Notice how short his answer is. He's in love with Hero, Leonato's short daughter.

CLAUDIO: If this is so, let him say it.

BENEDICK: Like the old tale, my lord, "It is not so, nor was it not so, but indeed, God forbid that it should be so!"

CLAUDIO: I hope to God my passions do not change.

DON PEDRO: Amen, if you love her, for the lady is very deserving of your love.

CLAUDIO: You say this to make sport of me, my lord.

DON PEDRO: No, on my word, I say what I think.

CLAUDIO: And, in faith, my lord, I spoke mine.

BENEDICK: And, by my two faiths and troths, my lord, I spoke mine.

CLAUDIO: That I love her, I feel.

180 DON PEDRO: That she is worthy, I know.

BENEDICK: That I neither feel how she should be loved, nor know
how she should be worthy, is the opinion that fire cannot
melt out of me. I will die in it at the stake.

DON PEDRO: Thou wast ever an obstinate heretic in the despite of
185 beauty.

CLAUDIO: And never could maintain his part but in the force of his
will.

BENEDICK: That a woman conceived me, I thank her; that she
brought me up, I likewise give her most humble thanks; but
190 that I will have a recheate winded in my forehead, or hang
my bugle in an invisible baldrick, all women shall pardon
me. Because I will not do them the wrong to mistrust any, I
will do myself the right to trust none; and the fine is, for the
which I may go the finer, I will live a bachelor.

195 DON PEDRO: I shall see thee, ere I die, look pale with love.

BENEDICK: With anger, with sickness, or with hunger, my lord; not
with love. Prove that ever I lose more blood with love than I
will get again with drinking, pick out mine eyes with a ballad-
maker's pen and hang me up at the door of a brothel house
200 for the sign of blind Cupid.

DON PEDRO: Well, if ever thou dost fall from this faith, thou wilt
prove a notable argument.

20

CLAUDIO: And, my lord, I honestly spoke my mind.

BENEDICK: And by both of my double faiths and trusts, sir, I spoke mine.

CLAUDIO: I feel that I love her.

DON PEDRO: I know that she is deserving.

BENEDICK: I neither feel that she should be loved, nor know that she is deserving. I would die at the stake in this opinion.

DON PEDRO: You always were stubborn in love.

CLAUDIO: And could never win except by sheer stubbornness.

BENEDICK: That a woman conceived me, I thank her; that she brought me up, I likewise give her thanks. However, women should excuse me—for no cuckhold's horns will be hung on my belt, nor their sound played upon my head. Since I will not accuse all women of infidelity, I won't disparage myself by trusting any. In conclusion, I will remain a bachelor.

DON PEDRO: Before I die, I will see you look sickly with love.

BENEDICK: With anger, with illness, or with hunger, sir, but not with love. If you prove that love will consume more of my blood than I gain by drinking, blind my eyes with a sonneteer's pen and hang me over a bordello's door as a sign of love.

DON PEDRO: Well, if you ever do falter in your faith regarding marriage, you will be a strong argument for it.

BENEDICK: If I do, hang me in a bottle like a cat and shoot at me; and he that hits me, let him be clapped on the shoulder and
205   called Adam.

DON PEDRO: Well, as time shall try. 'In time the savage bull doth bear the yoke.'

BENEDICK: The savage bull may; but if ever the sensible Benedick bear it, pluck off the bull's horns and set them in my fore-
210   head, and let me be vilely painted, and in such great letters as they write 'Here is good horse to hire,' let them signify under my sign. 'Here you may see Benedick the married man.'

CLAUDIO: If this should ever happen, thou wouldst be horn-mad.

DON PEDRO: Nay, if Cupid have not spent all his quiver in Venice,
215   thou wilt quake for this shortly.

BENEDICK: I look for an earthquake too, then.

DON PEDRO: Well, you will temporize with the hours. In the mean-time, good Signior Benedick, repair to Leonato's, commend me to him and tell him I will not fail him at supper; for
220   indeed he hath made great preparation.

BENEDICK: I have almost matter enough in me for such an embas-sage; and so I commit you—

CLAUDIO: To the tuition of God. From my house—if I had it—

DON PEDRO: The sixth of July. Your loving friend, Benedick.

BENEDICK: *If I ever do, put me in a cage like a cat and shoot arrows at me; anyone who hits me will be congratulated and called expert marksman.*

DON PEDRO: *Well, as the proverb says, "Even a savage bull can learn to carry a burden over time."*

BENEDICK: *A bull might, but if ever I do, remove the bull's horns and anchor them to my forehead, paint me wildly, and in huge letters write, as they do,'Here is a good horse to rent.' 'Here you may see Benedick the married man.'*

CLAUDIO: *If this would ever happen, you would certainly be mad with jealousy.*

DON PEDRO: *If Cupid has not used all his arrows in Venice, you will be wounded soon.*

BENEDICK: *I'm looking for an earthquake then, too.*

DON PEDRO: *Well, you will mellow with time. Meanwhile, good Benedick, go to Leonato's, greet him for me and tell him I'll arrive before supper since he has made great preparations.*

BENEDICK: *I have almost enough sense left in me for such a mission, and so I leave you—*

CLAUDIO: *To God's protection. From my house—if I had one—*

DON PEDRO: *The sixth of July. Your good friend, Benedick. [Claudio and Don Pedro are imitating very formal letters and Benedick's lack of facility in these matters].*

225 BENEDICK: Nay, mock not, mock not. The body of your discourse
is sometime guarded with fragments, and the guards are but
slightly basted on neither. Ere you flout old ends any further,
examine your conscience. And so I leave you.

[Exit.]

CLAUDIO: My liege, your highness now may do me good.

230 DON PEDRO: My love is thine to teach. Teach it but how,
And thou shalt see how apt it is to learn
Any hard lesson that may do thee good.

CLAUDIO: Hath Leonato any son, my lord?

DON PEDRO: No child but Hero; she's his only heir. Dost thou affect
235 her, Claudio?

CLAUDIO: O my lord,
When you went onward on this ended action,
I looked upon her with a soldier's eye,
That liked, but had a rougher task in hand
240 Than to drive liking to the name of love;
But now I am returned and that war-thoughts
Have left their places vacant, in their rooms
Come thronging soft and delicate desires,
All prompting me how fair young Hero is,
245 Saying I liked her ere I went to wars.

DON PEDRO: Thou wilt be like a lover presently
And tire the hearer with a book of words.
If thou dost love fair Hero, cherish it,
And I will break with her and with her father,
250 And thou shalt have her. Wast not to this end
That thou began'st to twist so fine a story?

BENEDICK: *Stop! Don't make fun of me. You are many times florid in speech. Before you mock me, look to your own speeches. Good-bye.*

[Exit Benedick.]

CLAUDIO: *My lord, you may now do me a favor.*

DON PEDRO: *Just show me how. Teach me the way and you will be pleased with how quick I am to help you.*

CLAUDIO: *Does Leonato have a son, my lord?*

DON PEDRO: *Hero is his only child, his only heir. Do you desire her, Claudio?*

CLAUDIO: *Sir, when I went off to battle, I viewed her with a soldier's eye. I liked her but had more important tasks to perform than to fall in love. Now, though, I have returned and thoughts of war are leaving my heart and in their place are soft and delicate desires all reminding me that I liked fair Hero before I left for war.*

DON PEDRO: *You will be like a lover soon and tire me with words of love. If you love her, cherish the idea. I will negotiate with her father and you will have her. Isn't this the ending you wanted to your story?*

CLAUDIO: How sweetly you do minister to love,
    That know love's grief by his complexion!
    But lest my liking might too sudden seem,
255   I would have salved it with a longer treatise.

DON PEDRO: What need the bridge much broader than the flood?
    The fairest grant is the necessity.
    Look, what will serve is fit.
    'Tis once, thou lovest,
260   And I will fit thee with the remedy.
    I know we shall have revelling to-night.
    I will assume thy part in some disguise
    And tell fair Hero I am Claudio,
    And in her bosom I'll unclasp my heart
265   And take her hearing prisoner with the force
    And strong encounter of my amorous tale.
    Then after to her father will I break;
    And the conclusion is, she shall be thine.
    In practice let us put it presently.

[Exeunt.]

monolouge

Scene 2
A Room in Leonato's House

[Enter Leonato and Antonio.]

LEONATO: How now, brother? Where is my cousin, your son? Hath
    he provided this music?

ANTONIO: He is very busy about it. But, brother, I can tell you
    strange news that you yet dreamt not of.

5   LEONATO: Are they good?

CLAUDIO: *How nicely you minister to love, since you could tell by my looks what the problem was. But as to not appear abrupt, I was prepared to talk at length on my feelings for her.*

DON PEDRO: *Why make the bridge much wider than the river? The best medicine is the one that is needed. See, what does the job is the best one. You are in love and I will get you a cure. We will be partying tonight where I will disguise myself as you, and tell Hero that I am Claudio; thus I will reveal my heart to her, and grab her heart with my story. Then, I will negotiate with her father. In conclusion, she will be yours. Let's do this immediately.*

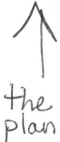

the
plan

[Exit.]

Scene 2
A Room in Leonato's House

[Enter Leonato and Antonio.]

LEONATO: *Hello, brother. Where is my nephew? Has he provided this music?*

ANTONIO: *He's busy with it now. But, brother I've got some news that you couldn't dream of.*

LEONATO: *Is it good news?*

ANTONIO: As the event stamps them; but they have a good cover, they show well outward. The prince and Count Claudio, walking in a thick-pleached alley in mine orchard, were thus much overheard by a man of mine; the prince discovered to
10   Claudio that he loved my niece your daughter and meant to acknowledge it this night in a dance, and if he found her accordant, he meant to take the present time by the top and instantly break with you of it.

LEONATO: Hath the fellow any wit that told you this?

15   ANTONIO: A good sharp fellow. I will send for him, and question him yourself.

LEONATO: No, no. We will hold it as a dream till it appear itself; but I will acquaint my daughter withal, that she may be the better prepared for an answer, if peradventure this be true. Go you
20   and tell her of it.

[Exit Antonio, Enter Antonio's son with a musician, and others.] Cousin, you know what you have to do. —[To the musician] O, I cry you mercy, friend. Go you with me, and I will use your skill.—Good cousin, have a care this busy time.

[Exeunt.]

Scene 3
Another Room in Leonato's House

[Enter Sir Don John and Conrade]

CONRADE: What the goodyear, my lord! Why are you thus out of measure sad?

DON JOHN: There is no measure in the occasion that breeds; therefore the sadness is without limit.

ANTONIO: *They seem outwardly pleasant as a good book bears an impressive cover. The prince and Claudio, walking in an overgrown avenue in my orchard, were overheard by my servant. The prince told Claudio that he loved Hero and would announce it at the dance tonight. If she agreed, he meant to seize the moment and quickly negotiate with you.*

LEONATO: *Is your servant trustworthy?*

ANTONIO: *He's very sharp. I'll send for him and you may question him yourself.*

LEONATO: *No. Let's just keep it a secret until it unfolds itself. But I will inform my daughter of these facts. If they are true, she will have a good answer prepared. Go and tell her of this.*

[Exit Antonio. Enter Antonio's son with a musician. Leonato to his nephew] Nephew, you know what you have to do. [To the musician] Please friend, come with me for I have need of your talents. Nephew, be careful during this busy time.

[Exit.]

Scene 3
Another Room in Leonato's House

[Enter Sir Don John and Conrade.]

CONRADE: *My lord, why are you so sad and miserable?*

DON JOHN: *There is no reason for it or this occasion that causes it, therefore, my sadness is without limit.*

5 CONRADE: You should hear reason.

DON JOHN: And when I have heard it, what blessings brings it?

CONRADE: If not a present remedy, at least a patient sufferance.

DON JOHN: I wonder that thou being, as thou say'st thou art, born
    under Saturn, goest about to apply a moral medicine to a
10   mortifying mischief. I cannot hide what I am: I must be sad
    when I have cause, and smile at no man's jests; eat when I
    have stomach, and wait for no man's leisure; sleep when I
    am drowsy, and tend on no man's business; laugh when I am
    merry, and claw no man in his humour.

15 CONRADE: Yea, but you must not make the full show of this till you
    may do it without controlment. You have of late stood out
    against your brother, and he hath ta'en you newly into his
    grace, whereit is impossible you should take true root but by
    the fair weather that you make yourself. It is needful that you
20   frame the season for your own harvest.

DON JOHN: I had rather be a canker in a hedge than a rose in his
    grace, and it better fits my blood to be disdained of all than
    to fashion a carriage to rob love from any. In this, though I
    cannot be said to be a flattering honest man, it must not be
25   denied but I am a plain-dealing villain. I am trusted with a
    muzzle and enfranchised with a clog; therefore I have decreed
    not to sing in my cage. If I had my mouth, I would bite; if I
    had my liberty, I would do my liking. In the meantime let me
    be that I am, and seek not to alter me.

30 CONRADE: Can you make no use of your discontent?

DON JOHN: I make all use of it, for I use it only. [Enter Borachio.]
    Who comes here? What news, Borachio?

BORACHIO: I came yonder from a great supper. The prince your
    brother is royally entertained by Leonato, and I can give you
35   intelligence of an intended marriage.

CONRADE: *You should hear logic.*

DON JOHN: *What good news would hearing logic bring?*

CONRADE: *If not a cure, at least an endurable pain.*

DON JOHN: *I wonder if you, [being born under an ill-disposed planet] mean to apply philosophy to my deadly disease. I cannot hide what I am. I must be sad when I have reason, smile at no man's jokes, eat when I am hungry, and wait on no man; sleep when I am drowsy, do no one else's job; laugh when I am happy, and flatter no man in his conceits.*

CONRADE: *Yes, but you must hide your feelings until you can do something openly about it. You recently were in rebellion against your brother, and he had taken you back into his good graces where you can prosper only by appearing docile. You must choose your revenge carefully.*

DON JOHN: *I would rather be a weed in the bushes than a rose in his garden. I'm happier as an outcast than in someone's favor. Although I cannot be called an honest man, it can't be denied that I am honestly a villain. I am shackled for now, but I won't sing in my captivity. If my mouth were free I would bite him, if I had my freedom I would do as I please. Meanwhile, leave me alone and don't try to change me.*

CONRADE: *Can't you find use for your unhappiness?*

DON JOHN: *I make all use of it since it is all I use. [Enter Borachio.] Who's there? What news do you bring, Borachio?*

BORACHIO: *I come from a great feast where your brother is royally entertained by Leonato; and I can tell you of an intended marriage.*

DON JOHN: Will it serve for any model to build mischief on? What is he for a fool that betroths himself to unquietness?

BORACHIO: Marry, it is your brother's right hand.

DON JOHN: Who? the most exquisite Claudio?

40 BORACHIO: Even he.

DON JOHN: A proper squire! And who? and who? which way looks he?

BORACHIO: Marry, on Hero, the daughter and heir of Leonato.

DON JOHN: A very forward March-chick! How came you to this?

45 BORACHIO: Being entertained for a perfumer, as I was smoking a musty room, comes me the prince and Claudio, hand in hand in sad conference. I whipt me behind the arras and there heard it agreed upon that the prince should woo Hero for himself, and having obtained her, give her to Count Claudio.

50 DON JOHN: Come, come, let us thither. This may prove food to my displeasure. That young start-up hath all the glory of my overthrow. If I can cross him any way, I bless myself every way. You are both sure, and will assist me?

CONRADE: To the death, my lord.

55 DON JOHN: Let us to the great supper. Their cheer is the greater that I am subdued. Would the cook were of my mind! Shall we go prove what's to be done?

BORACHIO: We'll wait upon your lordship.

[Exeunt.]

32

DON JOHN: Will it be an appropriate model to cause trouble with? Who is the fool who wants unpleasantness in his life?

BORACHIO: Why, it's your brother's right hand man.

DON JOHN: Who? [sarcastically] The great Claudio?

BORACHIO: Even so.

DON JOHN: A "fine" gentleman. Who does he look on?

BORACHIO: Why, on Hero, Leonato's heir and daughter.

DON JOHN: A precocious child! How did you find this out?

BORACHIO: I was hired to spread incense in the rooms at Leonato's. As I was perfuming a stale room, Claudio and the prince came in talking very seriously. I hid behind the tapestry and overheard them agree that the prince would woo Hero for himself, obtain her, and then give her to Claudio.

DON JOHN: Well, well! Let's go there. This may feed my discomfort. That young bootlicker has all the rewards of my defeat. If I can vex him in any way, I'll please myself. You are both sure, and will aid me?

CONRADE: To the death, sir.

DON JOHN: Let's go to the feast. They will be happier still, if I appear despondent. I wish the cook were of my mind! Should we go and see what mischief we can do?

BORACHIO: We're ready to aid you, sir.

[All Exit.]

Act II

Scene 1
A Hall in Leonato's House

[Enter Leonato, Antonio, Hero, Beatrice, and others.]

LEONATO: Was not Count Don John here at supper?

ANTONIO: I saw him not.

BEATRICE: How tartly that gentleman looks! I never can see him but
I am heart-burned an hour after.

5 HERO: He is of a very melancholy disposition.

BEATRICE: He were an excellent man that were made just in the
midway between him and Benedick. The one is too like an
image and says nothing, and the other too like my lady's
eldest son, evermore tattling.

10 LEONATO: Then half Signior Benedick's tongue in Count Don John's
mouth, and half Count Don John's melancholy in Signior
Benedick's face—

BEATRICE: With a good leg and a good foot, uncle, and money
enough in his purse, such a man would win any woman in
15 the world—if 'a could get her good will.

Act II

Scene 1
A Hall in Leonato's House

[Enter Leonato, Antonio, Hero, Beatrice, and others.]

LEONATO: Wasn't Count Don John here at supper?

ANTONIO: I didn't see him.

BEATRICE: How sour Count John looks. I can never see him without having indigestion an hour later.

HERO: He certainly has a melancholy personality.

BEATRICE: A man midway between him and Benedick would be excellent. The one is too much like a silent statue, and the other is too talkative, like a babbling child.

LEONATO: So, half of Signior Benedick's tongue in Don John's mouth, and half of the count's disposition in Signior Benedick's face—

BEATRICE: Well, uncle, with a good physique and a good technique, and with ready money in his pocket, such a man could win the heart of any woman—if he could please her.

LEONATO: By my troth, niece, thou wilt never get thee a husband if thou be so shrewd of thy tongue.

ANTONIO: In faith, she's too curst.

20 BEATRICE: Too curst is more than curst. I shall lessen God's sending that way, for it is said, 'God sends a curst cow short horns'; but to a cow too curst he sends none.

LEONATO: So, by being too curst, God will send you no horns.

BEATRICE: Just, if he send me no husband; for the which blessing I am at him upon my knees every morning and evening. Lord, 25 I could not endure a husband with a beard on his face. I had rather lie in the woollen!

LEONATO: You may light on a husband that hath no beard.

BEATRICE: What should I do with him? dress him in my apparel and make him my waiting gentlewoman? He that hath a beard is more than a youth, and he that hath no beard is less than a 30 man; and he that is more than a youth is not for me; and he that is less than a man, I am not for him. Therefore I will even take sixpence in earnest of the bear-ward and lead his apes into hell.

LEONATO: Well then, go you into hell?

35 BEATRICE: No; but to the gate, and there will the devil meet me like an old cuckold with horns on his head, and say 'Get you to heaven, Beatrice, get you to heaven. Here's no place for you maids.' So deliver I up my apes, and away to Saint Peter—for the heavens. He shows me where the bachelors sit, and there 40 live we as merry as the day is long.

ANTONIO: [to Hero] Well, niece, I trust you will be ruled by your father.

LEONATO: Honestly, niece, you'll never get a husband if you are so sarcastic.

ANTONIO: Truly, she's too shrewish.

BEATRICE: Too shrewish is more than shrewish. I'll save God the trouble, for it is said, "God sends a shrew a small man," but to a very shrewish woman he sends none.

LEONATO: So being very shrewish, God will send you no horns.

BEATRICE: Just if he sends me no husband, for which I thank God on my knees every morning and night. Lord, I couldn't stand a bearded husband. I'd rather lie on woolen blankets!

LEONATO: You may find a husband who doesn't have a beard.

BEATRICE: What could I do with him? Would I dress him in my clothes and make him my female attendant? A man with a beard is more than a boy, and he that doesn't have a beard is less than a man; and he that is more than a boy is not for me, and he that is less than a man, I am not for him. Therefore, I take money from the animal trainer and lead his apes into hell.

LEONATO: Well then, are you going to go into hell?

BEATRICE: No, only to the gate where the devil will meet me dressed in horns and say 'Get you to heaven, Beatrice, get you to heaven. This is no place for virgins.' So I'll deliver him my apes, and go to heaven. There, St. Peter will show me where unmarried singles sit and we all will live merrily on.

ANTONIO: [In the pause, Antonio addresses Hero.] Hero, I hope that you will be governed by your father.

37

BEATRICE: Yes faith. It is my cousin's duty to make courtesy and say,
'Father, as it please you.' But yet for all that, cousin, let him
45   be a handsome fellow, or else make another courtesy, and say,
'Father, as it please me.'

LEONATO: Well, niece, I hope to see you one day fitted with a husband.

BEATRICE: Not till God make men of some other metal than earth.
50   Would it not grieve a woman to be overmastered with a
piece of valiant dust? to make an account of her life to a clod
of wayward marl? No, uncle, I'll none. Adam's sons are my
brethren, and truly I hold it a sin to match in my kindred.

LEONATO: Daughter, remember what I told you. If the prince do
55   solicit you in that kind, you know your answer.

BEATRICE: The fault will be in the music, cousin, if you be not
wooed in good time. If the prince be too important, tell him
there is measure in everything, and so dance out the answer.
For, hear me, Hero, wooing, wedding, and repenting is as
60   a Scotch jig, a measure, and a cinque-pace: the first suit is
hot and hasty like a Scotch jig—and full as fantastical; the
wedding, mannerly modest, as a measure, full of state and
ancientry; and then comes repentance and with his bad legs
falls into the cinque-pace faster and faster, till he sink into his
65   grave.

LEONATO: Cousin, you apprehend passing shrewdly.

BEATRICE: I have a good eye, uncle; I can see a church by daylight.

LEONATO: The revellers are entering, brother. Make good room.

BEATRICE: Indeed, it's my cousin's duty to curtsy and say, "Whatever will please you, father." However, cousin, let the man be handsome, or else curtsy and say, "Whatever will please me, father."

LEONATO: Well, niece, I still hope to see you married someday.

BEATRICE: Not until God makes men out of some substance besides earth. Wouldn't it be depressing for a woman to be subservient to a piece of dust? To spend her life with a clod of mud? No, uncle, I'll not wed. The sons of Adam are my kin, and honestly I think it a sin to wed a brother.

LEONATO: Daughter, remember what I told you. If the prince proposes, you know your answer.

BEATRICE: The mistake will be in the music, cousin, if you are not courted in proper time. If the Prince is too persistent, tell him there is moderation in everything and dance out your answer. Hear me, Hero. Courting, wedding, and repenting are like fast, moderate, and lively dances. Courting is quick and steamy and elusive, the wedding proper and moderate full of ceremony and civility. Then comes repenting where the man goes quicker and quicker, finally dying.

LEONATO: Beatrice, you perceive life shrewdly.

BEATRICE: I have good eyes, uncle; I can see a church clearly by daylight.

LEONATO: The guests are coming, brother. Give them some room.

[Enter Don Pedro, Don John, Borachio, Claudio, Benedick, Balthasar, Margaret, Ursula, and others, masked.]

DON PEDRO: Lady, will you walk about with your friend?

70 HERO: So you walk softly and look sweetly and say nothing, I am yours for the walk; and especially when I walk away.

DON PEDRO: With me in your company?

HERO: I may say so when I please.

DON PEDRO: And when please you to say so?

75 HERO: When I like your favour, for God defend the lute should be like the case!

DON PEDRO: My visor is Philemon's roof; within the house is Jove.

HERO: Why then, your visor should be thatched.

[Draws her aside.]

DON PEDRO: Speak low if you speak love.

BALTHASAR: Well, I would you did like me.

80 MARGARET: So would not I for your own sake, for I have many ill qualities.

BALTHASAR: Which is one?

MARGARET: I say my prayers aloud.

BALTHASAR: I love you the better. The hearers may cry Amen.

[Enter Don Pedro, Don John, Borachio, Claudio, Benedick, Balthasar, Margaret, Ursula, and others, masked.]

DON PEDRO: Miss, will you walk with me?

HERO: If you walk softly, look sweetly, and say nothing, I am yours
    for a walk, especially when I walk away.

DON PEDRO: Walk away with me?

HERO: I may if I please.

DON PEDRO: And when will that be?

HERO: If I like your face, since the instrument should be like the
    case it's put in.

DON PEDRO: My mask, like Jove when he was disguised as a peas-
    ant, holds no comparison to my god-like face.

HERO: Why then, your mask should be whiskered.

[Draws her to the side of the stage.]

DON PEDRO: Speak softly when you speak of love.

BALTHASAR: I hope you like me.

MARGARET: I hope you like me, too, since I have many bad traits.

BALTHASAR: Which is one?

MARGARET: I say my prayers aloud.

BALTHASAR: So much the better! Whoever hears you will cry
    Amen.

90 MARGARET: God match me with a good dancer!

BALTHASAR: Amen.

MARGARET: And God keep him out of my sight when the dance is
        done! Answer, clerk.

BALTHASAR: No more words. The clerk is answered.

        [Takes her aside.]

95 URSULA: I know you well enough. You are Signior Antonio.

ANTONIO: At a word, I am not.

URSULA: I know you by the waggling of your head.

ANTONIO: To tell you true, I counterfeit him.

URSULA: You could never do him so ill-well unless you were the
100   very man. Here's his dry hand up and down. You are he, you
        are he!

ANTONIO: At a word, I am not.

URSULA: Come, come, do you think I do not know you by your
        excellent wit? Can virtue hide itself? Go to, mum, you are he.
105   Graces will appear, and there's an end. [They step aside.]

BEATRICE: Will you not tell me who told you so?

BENEDICK: No, you shall pardon me.

BEATRICE: Nor will you not tell me who you are?

42

MARGARET: *I hope God matches me with a lively man.*

BALTHASAR: *Amen to that.*

MARGARET: *And I hope God keeps him away from me when the dance is done. What's your response?*

BALTHASAR: *No more words. I've been answered.*

[They step aside and are replaced by Ursula and Antonio.]

URSULA: *I know you well. You're Signior Antonio.*

ANTONIO: *Really, I'm not.*

URSULA: *I know you by the flapping of your head.*

ANTONIO: *Honestly, I'm imitating him.*

URSULA: *You couldn't do him so poorly unless you were he. The weathered hands are all chapped the same. You're he, you're he!*

ANTONIO: *Really, I'm not.*

URSULA: *Come on, don't you think I recognize your excellent humor? Can you hide such nobleness? Really, good qualities always rise to be noticed. [They step aside and are replaced by Beatrice and Benedick.]*

BEATRICE: *Will you tell me who told you that?*

BENEDICK: *No, you must pardon me.*

BEATRICE: *Nor will you tell me who you are?*

BENEDICK: Not now.

110 BEATRICE: That I was disdainful, and that I had my good wit out of the Hundred Merry Tales—well, this was Signior Benedick that said so.

BENEDICK: What's he?

BEATRICE: I am sure you know him well enough.

115 BENEDICK: Not I, believe me.

BEATRICE: Did he never make you laugh?

BENEDICK: I pray you, what is he?

BEATRICE: Why, he is the prince's jester, a very dull fool. Only his gift is in devising impossible slanders. None but libertines
120 delight in him; and the commendation is not in his wit, but in his villany; for he both pleases men and angers them, and then they laugh at him and beat him. I am sure he is in the fleet. I would he had boarded me.

BENEDICK: When I know the gentleman, I'll tell him what you say.

125 BEATRICE: Do, do. He'll but break a comparison or two on me; which peradventure, not marked or not laughed at, strikes him into melancholy; and then there's a partridge wing saved, for the fool will eat no supper that night. [Music.] We must follow the leaders.

130 BENEDICK: In every good thing.

BEATRICE: Nay, if they lead to any ill, I will leave them at the next turning.

BENEDICK: Not now.

BEATRICE: You were told that I was haughty and that I got my humor out of common joke books from Signior Benedick.

BENEDICK: Who is he?

BEATRICE: I'm sure you know him well enough.

BENEDICK: Not I, believe me.

BEATRICE: Didn't he ever make you laugh?

BENEDICK: Why? Who is he?

BEATRICE: Why he's the prince's jester, a dull buffoon. His only talent lies in making up incredible stories. None but over-sexed wastrels, like himself, care for him, and then only for his mischief, not his wit. Men both hate and like him since they laugh and beat him. I'm sure he's here, I wish he had approached me.

BENEDICK: When I meet the gentlemen, I'll tell him what you said.

BEATRICE: Please do. He'll only crack a joke or two about me; and when his remark is not received by laughter it will send him into a depression. Thus, the fool will have no appetite and a partridge wing may be saved from consumption. [Music begins again] Come, we must dance this way, following the leaders.

BENEDICK: Yes, in everything.

BEATRICE: No, if they lead poorly, I'll leave them at the next turning.

[Exeunt. All but Don John, Borachio, and Claudio dance.]

DON JOHN: Sure my brother is amorous on Hero and hath with-
drawn her father to break with him about it. The ladies follow
135 her and but one visor remains.

BORACHIO: And that is Claudio. I know him by his bearing.

DON JOHN: Are you not Signior Benedick?

CLAUDIO: You know me well. I am he.

DON JOHN: Signior, you are very near my brother in his love. He is
140 enamoured on Hero. I pray you dissuade him from her; she is
no equal for his birth. You may do the part of an honest man
in it.

CLAUDIO: How know you he loves her?

DON JOHN: I heard him swear his affection.

145 BORACHIO: So did I too, and he swore he would marry her tonight.

DON JOHN: Come, let us to the banquet.

[Exeunt Don John and Borachio.]

CLAUDIO: Thus answer I in name of Benedick,
But hear these ill news with the ears of Claudio.
'Tis certain so; the prince wooes for himself.
150 Friendship is constant in all other things
Save in the office and affairs of love.
Therefore all hearts in love use their own tongues;
let every eye negotiate for itself,
And trust no agent; for beauty is a witch
155 Against whose charms faith melteth into blood.
This is an accident of hourly proof,
Which I mistrusted not. Farewell therefore Hero!

[Exit. All but Don John, Borachio, and Claudio dance.]

DON JOHN: Indeed, my brother loves Hero and has left to negotiate with Leonato. The crowd follows her, but a lone figure remains there.

BORACHIO: That's Claudio. I know him by the way he carries himself.

DON JOHN: *[To Claudio]* Aren't you Signior Benedick?

CLAUDIO: You recognized me. I am he.

DON JOHN: Sir, you are close to my brother. Please persuade him not to marry Hero—whom he loves. She is not his equal. We need your honest help.

CLAUDIO: How do you know that he loves her?

DON JOHN: I heard him say it.

BORACHIO: So did I, and he swore he would propose tonight.

DON JOHN: Come, let's go to the feast.

[Exit Don John and Borachio.]

CLAUDIO: I answered to the name of Benedick *[taking his mask off]* but heard this bad news with my own ears. It's true. The prince woos for himself. Friendship transcends all endeavors except those concerning love. All hearts should use their own tongues in love, negotiate for themselves, and trust no one to do it for you. For beauty is a beguiler whose charms melt good intentions, and this misfortune of mine proves it. Farewell, Hero!

[Enter Benedick unmasked.]

BENEDICK: Count Claudio?

CLAUDIO: Yea, the same.

160   BENEDICK: Come, will you go with me?

CLAUDIO: Whither?

BENEDICK: Even to the next willow, about your own business,
county. What fashion will you wear the garland of? about
your neck, like an usurer's chain? or under your arm, like a
165   lieutenant's scarf? You must wear it one way, for the prince
hath got your Hero.

CLAUDIO: I wish him joy of her.

BENEDICK: Why, that's spoken like an honest drovier. So they sell
bullocks. But did you think the prince would have served you
170   thus?

CLAUDIO: I pray you leave me.

BENEDICK: Ho! now you strike like the blind man! 'Twas the boy
that stole your meat, and you'll beat the post.

CLAUDIO: If it will not be, I'll leave you.

[Exit.]

175   BENEDICK: Alas, poor hurt fowl! now will he creep into sedges. But,
that my Lady Beatrice should know me, and not know me!
The prince's fool! Ha! it may be I go under that title because I
am merry. Yea, but so I am apt to do myself wrong. I am not
so reputed. It is the base though bitter, disposition of Beatrice
180   that puts the world into her person and so gives me out. Well,
I'll be revenged as I may.

48

[Benedick enters without a mask.]

BENEDICK: Count Claudio?

CLAUDIO: Yes, that's me.

BENEDICK: Will you come with me?

CLAUDIO: Where?

BENEDICK: How about to the nearest willow to fashion you a ribbon. Should we put it around your neck like a money-lender's chain? How about under your arm like a soldier's scarf? You have to wear it somewhere since the prince has stolen your Hero.

CLAUDIO: I hope he's happy with her.

BENEDICK: Why that's spoken like an honest cattle salesman. That is how they sell bulls. Did you ever think the prince would have done this to you?

CLAUDIO: Please, leave me alone.

BENEDICK: What! Now you lash out like a blind man wildly beating the post when it was the boy who stole your meat.

CLAUDIO: If you won't leave me, I'll leave you.

[He exits.]

BENEDICK: Poor bird, he'll now hide in a hedge. The prince's jester! Well, it might be I have that name because I'm happy. Maybe, but that belittles me. I don't have that reputation. It's Beatrice's bitter personality which has turned people against me. Well, I'll get my revenge.

49

[Enter Don Pedro.]

DON PEDRO: Now, signior, where's the count? Did you see him?

BENEDICK: Troth, my lord, I have played the part of Lady Fame. I
found him here as melancholy as a lodge in a warren. I told
185   him, and I think I told him true, that your grace had got
the good will of this young lady, and I offered him my company to a willow tree, either to make him a garland, as being
forsaken, or to bind him up a rod, as being worthy to be
whipped.

DON PEDRO: To be whipped? What's his fault?

190   BENEDICK: The flat transgression of a schoolboy who, being overjoyed with finding a bird's nest, shows it his companion, and
he steals it.

DON PEDRO: Wilt thou make a trust a transgression? The transgression is in the stealer.

195   BENEDICK: Yet it had not been amiss the rod had been made, and
the garland too; for the garland he might have worn himself,
and the rod he might have bestowed on you, who, as I take it,
have stolen his birds' nest.

200   DON PEDRO: I will but teach them to sing and restore them to the
owner.

BENEDICK: If their singing answer your saying, by my faith, you say
honestly.

DON PEDRO: The Lady Beatrice hath a quarrel to you. The gentleman that danced with her told her she is much wronged by
205   you.

BENEDICK: O, she misused me past the endurance of a block! An oak
but with one green leaf on it would have answered her; my

[Enter Don Pedro.]

DON PEDRO: *Sir, where's the count? Have you seen him?*

BENEDICK: *Yes, my lord, I have borne tidings to him. I found him as unhappy as a rabbit in his hole. I told him, and I honestly believe, that you have the heart of Hero. I offered him my company to the nearest willow to either dress him in ribbons or to make him a whip to be beaten with.*

DON PEDRO: *To be whipped? What is his mistake?*

BENEDICK: *The error of a schoolboy who, overjoyed at finding a bird's nest, shows it to his companion, and the friend steals it.*

DON PEDRO: *Is faith in someone a fault? The fault is in the thief.*

BENEDICK: *It's too bad we didn't make both the whip and the ribbon. The ribbon he might have worn himself, and the whip he might have used on you; since, as I understand it, you have taken his bird's nest.*

DON PEDRO: *I will teach these birds to sing and bring them together.*

BENEDICK: *If this turns out as you say, then you have spoken honestly.*

DON PEDRO: *Lady Beatrice is upset with you. One gentleman who danced with her told her that you have slandered her.*

BENEDICK: *Oh, she has mightily abused me. A near-dead tree would have spoken against her. My own mask assumed life and scolded her. She told me, mistaking me for another, that*

51

very visor began to assume life and scold with her. She told
me, not thinking I had been myself, that I was the prince's
210   jester, that I was duller than a great thaw; huddling jest upon
jest with such impossible conveyance upon me that I stood
like a man at a mark, with a whole army shooting at me. She
speaks poniards, and every word stabs. If her breath were as
terrible as her terminations, there were no living near her; she
215   would infect to the North Star. I would not marry her though
she were endowed with all that Adam had left him before he
transgressed. She would have made Hercules have turned spit,
yea, and have cleft his club to make the fire too. Come, talk
not of her. You shall find her the infernal Ate in good apparel.
220   I would to God some scholar would conjure her, for certainly,
while she is here, a man may live as quiet in hell as in a sanc-
tuary; and people sin upon purpose, because they would go
thither; so indeed all disquiet, horror, and perturbation follows her.

[Enter Claudio, Beatrice, Leonato, and Hero.]

225   DON PEDRO: Look, here she comes.

BENEDICK: Will your Grace command me any service to the world's
end? I will go on the slightest errand now to the Antipodes
that you can devise to send me on; I will fetch you a tooth-
picker now from the furthest inch of Asia; bring you the
230   length of Prester Don John's foot; fetch you a hair off the great
Cham's beard; do you any embassage to the Pygmies—rather
than hold three words' conference with this harpy. You have
no employment for me?

DON PEDRO: None, but to desire your good company.

235   BENEDICK: O God, my lord, here's a dish I love not! I cannot endure
my Lady Tongue.

[Exit.]

I was the prince's fool; that I was duller than a housebound day. She heaped abuse upon abuse with such dexterity that I felt like a man in front of an army at target practice. She throws verbal darts at me, and every one hurts. If her breath were as bad as her name-calling, nothing could live near her; she would smell to the heavens. I wouldn't marry her if she had all the riches there ever were since Adam's time. She would have given Hercules menial jobs! Now, let's not talk of her. She's too like the goddess of discord. I wish someone could make her disappear. Certainly, when she is around, hell seems as quiet as a monastery and people sin intentionally so they can go there and avoid the noise and confusion that follow her.

[Enter Claudio, Beatrice, Leonato, and Hero.]

DON PEDRO: *Look, here she comes.*

BENEDICK: *Would you please send me on an errand to the world's end? I will go on the smallest mission you can devise for me, fetching a toothpick from farthest Asia, bringing home the length of the Emperor John's foot, stealing a hair from the Mongol Ruler's beard. Send me to negotiate with the pygmies in far off India—anything rather than to talk with this harpy. Do you not have a job for me to do?*

DON PEDRO: *Only that you stay and keep us company.*

BENEDICK: *God, sir, here's a food I do not love! I cannot stomach my Lady Tongue.*

[Exit.]

53

DON PEDRO: Come, lady, come; you have lost the heart of Signior
Benedick.

BEATRICE: Indeed, my lord, he lent it me awhile, and I gave him use
240   for it—a double heart for his single one. Marry, once before
he won it of me with false dice; therefore your Grace may well
say I have lost it.

DON PEDRO: You have put him down, lady; you have put him down.

BEATRICE: So I would not he should do me, my lord, lest I should
245   prove the mother of fools. I have brought Count Claudio,
whom you sent me to seek.

DON PEDRO: Why, how now, count? Wherefore are you sad?

CLAUDIO: Not sad, my lord.

DON PEDRO: How then? sick?

250 CLAUDIO: Neither, my lord.

BEATRICE: The count is neither sad, nor sick, nor merry, nor well;
but civil count—civil as an orange, and something of that
jealous complexion.

DON PEDRO: I' faith, lady, I think your blazon to be true; though
255   I'll be sworn, if he be so, his conceit is false. Here, Claudio, I
have wooed in thy name, and fair Hero is won. I have broke
with her father, and his good will obtained. Name the day of
marriage, and God give thee joy!

DON PEDRO: *Well, lady, you've lost Signior Benedick's heart.*

BEATRICE: *Yes, sir, he lent it to me for a while, and I gave him my heart doubly for his single one. Yes, he once won my heart with trickery, so you may say that I have lost it.*

DON PEDRO: *You've put him down, Beatrice; you've put him down.*

BEATRICE: *Yes, so that he wouldn't do it to me, sir. Otherwise, I would be the mother of idiots. [Changing the subject.] As you requested, I have returned with Claudio.*

DON PEDRO: *Hello, Count Claudio, why are you sad?*

CLAUDIO: *I'm not sad, my lord.*

DON PEDRO: *Well, then, are you sick?*

CLAUDIO: *Neither, my lord.*

BEATRICE: *Claudio is not sick, not sad, not happy, not well, but a sober count, sober as an orange and with a similar jealous complexion.*

DON PEDRO: *In truth, lady, I think your description is accurate, though I'd swear that his reason for being upset is not true. Come, Claudio, I have wooed Hero for you and won her heart. I have bargained with Leonato and he has consented. Name the day of your marriage, and God grant you happiness!*

LEONATO: Count, take of me my daughter, and with her my for-
260   tunes. His Grace hath made the match, and all grace say
           Amen to it!

BEATRICE: Speak, count, 'tis your cue.

CLAUDIO: Silence is the perfectest herald of joy. I were but little
           happy if I could say how much. Lady, as you are mine, I
265   am yours. I give away myself for you and dote upon the
           exchange.

BEATRICE: Speak, cousin; or, if you cannot, stop his mouth with a
           kiss and let not him speak neither.

DON PEDRO: In faith, lady, you have a merry heart.

270 BEATRICE: Yea, my lord; I thank it, poor fool, it keeps on the windy
           side of care. My cousin tells him in his ear that he is in her
           heart.

CLAUDIO: And so she doth, cousin.

BEATRICE: Good Lord, for alliance! Thus goes every one to the
275   world but I, and I am sunburnt. I may sit in a corner and cry
           'Heigh-ho for a husband!'

DON PEDRO: Lady Beatrice, I will get you one.

BEATRICE: I would rather have one of your father's getting. Hath
           your Grace neer a brother like you? Your father got excellent
280   husbands, if a maid could come by them.

DON PEDRO: Will you have me, lady?

BEATRICE: No, my lord, unless I might have another for working

LEONATO: *Here, Claudio, take my daughter's hand and my fortune. The prince has made the match, and God may say Amen to it.*

BEATRICE: *Speak, count, it's your line.*

CLAUDIO: *Silence is the outward show of such joy. I can't begin to tell you how happy I am. Hero, as you are mine, I am yours. I give myself to you and am overjoyed.*

BEATRICE: *Please, Hero, say something; or if you can't, kiss him so he can't speak either.*

DON PEDRO: *Why, Beatrice, you have a humorous disposition.*

BEATRICE: *Yes, my lord. I thank its innocence for keeping me clear of danger. Look, Hero whispers to Claudio that he is loved deeply.*

CLAUDIO: *She certainly does, cousin.*

BEATRICE: *Thank God for marriage! Everyone in the world is getting married, but I'm no longer fair. I may sit in a corner and cry "Heigh-ho for a husband."*

DON PEDRO: *Lady Beatrice, I'll get you one.*

BEATRICE: *I'd rather have one of your father's getting. Does your highness have a brother like you? Your father has excellent husbands for heirs, if a woman could come by one.*

DON PEDRO: *Will you marry me, miss?*

BEATRICE: *No, my lord, unless I could have another for everyday;*

57

285 days: your Grace is too costly to wear every day. But I beseech your Grace pardon me. I was born to speak all mirth and no matter.

DON PEDRO: Your silence most offends me, and to be merry best becomes you, for out o' question you were born in a merry hour.

290 BEATRICE: No, sure, my lord, my mother cried; but then there was a star danced, and under that was I born. Cousins, God give you joy!

LEONATO: Niece, will you look to those things I told you of?

BEATRICE: I cry you mercy, uncle, By your Grace's pardon.

[Exit.]

DON PEDRO: By my troth, a pleasant-spirited lady.

295 LEONATO: There's little of the melancholy element in her, my lord. She is never sad but when she sleeps; and not ever sad then; for I have heard my daughter say she hath often dreamt of unhappiness and waked herself with laughing.

DON PEDRO: She cannot endure to hear tell of a husband.

300 LEONATO: O, by no means! She mocks all her wooers out of suit.

DON PEDRO: She were an excellent wife for Benedick.

LEONATO: O Lord, my lord! if they were but a week married, they would talk themselves mad.

DON PEDRO: County Claudio, when mean you to go to church?

your Grace is too expensive to wear every day. But, excuse me. I was born to say humorous things, not weighty ones.

Don Pedro: *Your silence would offend me more, and to be happy becomes you; for, honestly, you were born in a happy hour.*

Beatrice: *No, for sure, my lord, my mother cried, but then a star danced, and under it I was born. Cousins, may God give you joy!*

Leonato: *Niece, will you take care of those things I told you?*

Beatrice: *Excuse me, uncle. Pardon me, sir.*

[Exit Beatrice.]

Don Pedro: *Indeed, what a pleasant lady.*

Leonato: *There is little of unhappiness in her, my lord. She isn't even sad when she sleeps, for I have heard Hero say that Beatrice would often wake laughing from unhappy dreams.*

Don Pedro: *She just cannot endure talk of a husband.*

Leonato: *To be sure! She makes fun of all her suitors.*

Don Pedro: *She would be an excellent wife for Benedick.*

Leonato: *Good God, my lord! They would talk themselves crazy if they were married for only a week.*

Don Pedro: *Count Claudio, when do you mean to be married?*

305   CLAUDIO: To-morrow, my lord. Time goes on crutches till love have
           all his rites.

         LEONATO: Not till Monday, my dear son, which is hence just seven-
           night; and a time too brief too, to have all things answer my
           mind.

310   DON PEDRO: Come, you shake the head at so long a breathing; but I
           warrant thee, Claudio, the time shall not go dully by us. I will
           in the interim undertake one of Hercules' labours, which is,
           to bring Signior Benedick and the Lady Beatrice into a moun-
           tain of affection the one with the other. I would fain have it a
315   match, and I doubt not but to fashion it if you three will but
           minister such assistance as I shall give you direction.

         LEONATO: My lord, I am for you, though it cost me ten nights'
           watchings.

         CLAUDIO: And I, my lord.

320   DON PEDRO: And you too, gentle Hero?

         HERO: I will do any modest office, my lord, to help my cousin to a
           good husband.

         DON PEDRO: And Benedick is not the unhopefullest husband that
           I know. Thus far can I praise him: he is of a noble strain,
325   of approved valour, and confirmed honesty. I will teach you
           how to humour your cousin, that she shall fall in love with
           Benedick; and I, [to Leonato and Claudio] with your two
           helps, will so practice on Benedick that, in despite of his
           quick wit and his queasy stomach, he shall fall in love with
330   Beatrice. If we can do this Cupid is no longer an archer; his
           glory shall be ours, for we are the only love-gods. Go in with
           me, and I will tell you my drift.

                                      [Exeunt.]

CLAUDIO: Tomorrow, sir. Time goes slowly until I can consummate my marriage.

LEONATO: No, Claudio, not until Monday, which is only seven days away. Even that is too brief a time to plan all things as I wish.

DON PEDRO: Claudio, you shake your head at so long a wait, but I promise that the time will go quickly. I will undertake in the meantime a labor of Herculean proportions by bringing Benedick and Beatrice into love with each other. I can do this, but I need the help of you three as I direct you.

LEONATO: My lord, I will help you, even if it cost me ten nights of waiting.

CLAUDIO: And I, my lord.

DON PEDRO: And you, too, gentle Hero?

HERO: I will do any honest thing, my lord, to get a good husband for my cousin.

DON PEDRO: Benedick isn't the worst husband-material I've known. I can honestly say he is noble, courageous, and honest. I'll show Hero the way to trick Beatrice into loving Benedick and we males will trick Benedick, despite his nature, to fall in love with Beatrice. If we can do this, Cupid will have competition; his glory will be ours, and we will be love-gods. Come with me and I will tell you my plan.

[All Exit.]

61

Scene 2
A Hall in Leonato's House

[Enter Don John and Borachio.]

DON JOHN: It is so. The Count Claudio shall marry the daughter of Leonato.

BORACHIO: Yea, my lord; but I can cross it.

5 DON JOHN: Any bar, any cross, any impediment will be medicinable to me. I am sick in displeasure to him, and whatsoever comes athwart his affection ranges evenly with mine. How canst thou cross this marriage?

BORACHIO: Not honestly, my lord, but so covertly that no dishonesty shall appear in me.

10 DON JOHN: Show me briefly how.

BORACHIO: I think I told your lordship, a year since, how much I am in the favour of Margaret, the waiting gentlewoman to Hero.

DON JOHN: I remember.

15 BORACHIO: I can, at any unseasonable instant of the night, appoint her to look out at her lady's chamber window.

DON JOHN: What life is in that to be the death of this marriage?

BORACHIO: The poison of that lies in you to temper. Go you to the prince your brother; spare not to tell him that he hath
20 wronged his honour in marrying the renowned Claudio whose estimation do you mightily hold up, to a contaminated stale, such a one as Hero.

62

Scene 2
A Hall in Leonato's House

[Enter Don John and Borachio.]

DON JOHN: It's true. Claudio will marry Hero.

BORACHIO: Yes, sir, but I can ruin it.

DON JOHN: Any obstacle will be like a medicine for me. I am so sick with disgust towards Claudio that whoever can upset his plans will cure my ills. How can you impede this marriage?

BORACHIO: Not honestly, my lord; but with such cunning that no one will suspect me.

DON JOHN: Show me briefly, how?

BORACHIO: I think I told you how much Margaret, Hero's gentle-woman, loves me.

DON JOHN: I remember.

BORACHIO: I can, at anytime, have her step out on the balcony at Hero's window.

DON JOHN: How will this ruin the marriage?

BORACHIO: The ruin must be yours to apply. Go to Don Pedro and tell him that he has misused Claudio by arranging his marriage to a loose woman like Hero.

63

Don John: What proof shall I make of that?

Borachio: Proof enough to misuse the prince, to vex Claudio, to
25   undo Hero, and kill Leonato. Look you for any other issue?

Don John: Only to despite them I will endeavour anything.

Borachio: Go then; find a meet hour to draw Don Pedro and the
      Count Claudio alone; tell them that you know that Hero loves
      me; intend a kind of zeal both to the prince and Claudio,
30   as—in love of your brother's honour, who hath made this
      match, and his friend's reputation, who is thus like to be coz-
      ened with the semblance of a maid—that you have discovered
      thus. They will scarcely believe this without trial. Offer them
      instances; which shall bear no less likelihood than to see me
35   at her chamber window, hear me call Margaret, Hero, hear
      Margaret term me Claudio[1]; and bring them to see this the
      very night before the intended wedding—for in the meantime
      I will so fashion the matter that Hero shall be absent—and
      there shall appear such seeming truth of Hero's disloyalty that
40   jealousy shall be called assurance and all the preparation over-
      thrown.

Don John: Grow this to what adverse issue it can, I will put it in
      practice. Be cunning in the working this, and thy fee is a
      thousand ducats.

45 Borachio: Be you constant in the accusation, and my cunning shall
      not shame me.

Don John: I will presently go learn their day of marriage.

                                          [Exeunt.]

1.   *Some critics suggest this should read Borachio, since Claudio will overhear the*
     conversation.

DON JOHN: *What proof will I have of that?*

BORACHIO: *You can prove it enough to upset Don Pedro, spite Claudio, ruin Hero and kill Leonato. Isn't that enough?*

DON JOHN: *To get even with them I'll do anything.*

BORACHIO: *Go then and meet Claudio and Don Pedro; tell them that Hero loves me. In so doing, be sure to appear to be their friend,—who speaks only to save your brother's honor and Claudio's reputation, both of whom who have been deceived by the outward appearance of a virgin—and that you have discovered this. They will need proof to believe this. Offer them proof, which will be to see me at her bedroom window, hear me call her Hero, hear her call me Claudio, and bring them to this scene on the night before their intended wedding—I will make sure Hero is not present—and it will appear that Hero is disloyal. In that way there's sure to be jealousy, and the marriage preparations will be undone.*

DON JOHN: *No matter how large this conspiracy grows, I will put it into practice. Be skilled in your part and you will gain 1,000 gold coins.*

BORACHIO: *Make sure of your part, and my skill will not let you down.*

DON JOHN: *I'll go now and find out when they narry.*

[All Exit.]

Scene 3
Leonato's Garden

[Enter Benedick alone.]

BENEDICK: [Enter Boy.] Boy!

BOY: Signior?

BENEDICK: In my chamber window lies a book. Bring it hither to me
in the orchard.

5 BOY: I am here already, my lord.

BENEDICK: I know that, but I would have thee hence and here again.
[Exit Boy.] I do much wonder that one man, seeing how
much another man is a fool when he dedicates his behaviours
to love, will, after he hath laughed at such shallow follies in
10 others, become the argument of his own scorn by falling in
love; and such a man is Claudio. I have known when there
was no music with him but the drum and the fife; and now
had he rather hear the tabor and the pipe. I have known when
he would have walked ten mile afoot to see a good armour;
15 and now will he lie ten nights awake carving the fashion of
a new doublet. He was wont to speak plain and to the purpose, like an honest man and a soldier; and now is he turned
orthography; his words are a very fantastical banquet—just
so many strange dishes. May I be so converted and see with
20 these eyes? I cannot tell; I think not. I will not be sworn but
love may transform me to an oyster; but I'll take my oath on
it, till he have made an oyster of me he shall never make me
such a fool. One woman is fair, yet I am well; another is wise,
yet I am well; another virtuous, yet I am well; but till all grac-
25 es be in one woman, one woman shall not come in my grace.
Rich she shall be, that's certain; wise, or I'll none; virtuous, or
I'll never cheapen her; fair, or I'll never look on her; mild, or
come not near me; noble, or not I for an angel; of good discourse, an excellent musician, and her hair shall be of what

Scene 3
Leonato's Garden

[Enter Benedick alone.]

BENEDICK: *[Enter a young servant.] Boy!*

BOY: *Signior?*

BENEDICK: *There's a book in my bedroom window. Bring it to me in the orchard.*

BOY: *But, my lord, I'm already here.*

BENEDICK: *I know that, but I want you to go there and then come back. [Exit Boy.] I do wonder how foolish a man is when after laughing at the shallow behaviors of others who marry, he himself falls in love and thus becomes the object of his own sarcasm. Such a man is Claudio. I have known when he only heard the music of war drums, and now he would rather listen to soft music. I have known when he would have walked ten miles to see a fine suit of armor, and now he will lie awake ten nights designing a new set of clothes. He used to speak plainly and to the point like an honest soldier, and now he is enamored of words, with the words being a fantastic feast of very many weird dishes. Could I become like this? I don't know; I don't think so. It may be that love can change me into a fool, but I vow that I'll never act foolish until that happens. While one woman is fair, I am well; another is wise, yet I am well; another is virtuous, yet I am well; but until all attributes are found in one woman, one woman will not be found with me. She must be rich, that's for sure; wise or I'll have none of her; virtuous or I'll never bargain for her; fair, or I'll not look upon her; meek or she won't come near me; noble or I'll not have her for riches; an excellent musician, a*

67

30   colour it please God. Ha, the prince and Monsieur Love! I will
      hide me in the arbour. [Hides.]

[Enter Don Pedro, Leonato, Claudio. Music within.]

Don Pedro: Come, shall we hear this music?

Claudio: Yea, my good lord. How still the evening is, as hushed on
      purpose to grace harmony!

35   Don Pedro: See you where Benedick hath hid himself?

Claudio: O, very well, my lord. The music ended, We'll fit the kid-
      fox with a pennyworth.

[Enter Balthasar with Music.]

Don Pedro: Come, Balthasar, we'll hear that song again.

Balthasar: O, good my lord, tax not so bad a voice To slander
40   music any more than once.

Don Pedro: It is the witness still of excellency
          To put a strange face on his own perfection.
          I pray thee, sing, and let me woo no more.

Balthasar: Because you talk of wooing, I will sing;
45   Since many a wooer doth commence his suit
          To her he thinks not worthy, yet he wooes,
          Yet he will swear he loves.

Don Pedro: Nay, pray thee, come;
          Or, if thous wild hold no longer argument,
50   Do it in notes.

good speaker—and her hair shall be of whatever color that it please God. Ha! Here comes the prince and "Signior Love." I'll hide myself in the bushes.

[Enter Don Pedro, Leonato, Claudio. The sound of music can be heard coming from within the house.]

DON PEDRO: Come, let's hear this music.

CLAUDIO: Yes, my lord. How still the evening is, as if hushed on purpose to add to our good feeling.

DON PEDRO: Do you see where Benedick has hidden himself?

CLAUDIO: Indeed, my lord. The music has ended. Let's give the sly devil more than he bargained for.

[Enter Balthasar with Music.]

DON PEDRO: Here, Balthasar, let's hear that song again.

BALTHASAR: Please, my lord do not make my bad voice insult music any more than once.

DON PEDRO: Excellency still claims its own perfection is not. Please, sing, and let me love no more.

BALTHASAR: Since you talk of love, I will sing. Many a lover begins courting the wrong person but continues and swears love is true.

DON PEDRO: No more argument, but, if you must, sing it.

BALTHASAR: Note this before my notes;
            There's not a note of mine that's worth noting.

DON PEDRO: Why, these are very crotches that he speaks;
            Note, notes, forsooth, and nothing.   [Air]

55   BENEDICK: Now, divine air! now is his souls ravished! Is it not
            strange that sheeps' guts should hale souls out of men's
            bodies? Well, a horn for my money, when all's done.

BALTHASAR: The Song.

            Sigh no more, ladies, sigh no more,
60   Men were deceivers ever,
            One foot in sea and one on shore,
               To one thing constant never:

            Then sigh not so, but let them go,
               And be you blithe and bonny,
65   Converting all your sounds of woe
               Into Hey nonny, nonny.

            Sing no more ditties, sing no moe,
               Of dumps so dull and heavey;
            The fraud of men was ever so,
               Since summer first was leavy:
70   Then sigh not so,&c.

DON PEDRO: By my troth, a good song.

BALTHASAR: And an ill singer, my lord.

DON PEDRO: Ha, no, no, faith! Thou singest well enough for a shift.

BALTHASAR: *Note this before I begin my song: No notes of mine are worth noticing.*

DON PEDRO: *Why, this is music he speaks, all with "N's."*

BENEDICK: *Now, beautiful sounds! He reveals his tortured soul! Things as gross as sheep intestines call men's souls from their bodies: very odd. Anyway, my money's worth a sheep horn.*

BALTHASAR: *The Song.*

> *Sigh no more, ladies, sigh no more,*
>   *Men were deceivers ever,*
> *One foot in sea and one on shore,*
>   *To one thing constant never:*
>
> *Then sigh not so, but let them go,*
>   *And be you blithe and bonny,*
> *Converting all your sounds of woe*
>   *Into Hey nonny, nonny.*
>
> *Sing no more ditties, sing no moe,*
>   *Of dumps so dull and heavey;*
> *The fraud of men was ever so,*
>   *Since summer first was leavy:*
> *Then sigh not so,&c.*

DON PEDRO: *Truly, a pretty song.*

BALTHASAR: *And a poor singer, my lord.*

DON PEDRO: *No, no, indeed. You sing well enough for an emergency.*

BENEDICK: [Aside] An he had been a dog that should have howled
75   thus, they would have hanged him; and I pray God his bad
        voice bode no mischief. I had as live have heard the night
        raven, come what plague could have come after it.

DON PEDRO: Yea, marry. Dost thou hear, Balthasar? I pray thee get
        us some excellent music; for to-morrow night we would have
80   it at the Lady Hero's chamber window.

BALTHASAR: The best I can, my lord.

DON PEDRO: Do so. Farewell. [Exit Balthasar.] Come hither,
        Leonato. What was it you told me of to-day? that your niece
        Beatrice was in love with Signior Benedick?

85 CLAUDIO: O, ay! [Aside to Don Pedro] Stalk on, stalk on; the fowl
        sits. —I did never think that lady would have loved any man.

LEONATO: No, nor I neither; but most wonderful that she should
        so dote on Signior Benedick, whom she hath in all outward
        behaviours seemed ever to abhor.

BENEDICK: [Aside] Is't possible? Sits the wind in that corner?

90 LEONATO: By my troth, my lord, I cannot tell what to think of it,
        but that she loves him with an enraged affection. It is past the
        infinite of thought.

DON PEDRO: May be she doth but counterfeit.

CLAUDIO: Faith, like enough.

95 LEONATO: O God, counterfeit? There was never counterfeit of
        passion came so near the life of passion as she discovers it.

72

Benedick: [Aside] If a dog had howled like this, they would have killed him. I hope to God that this pitiful voice doesn't indicate future trouble. I would just as soon have heard harbingers of death and plague as this.

Don Pedro: Yes, Balthasar. Do you hear? I want you to find us some beautiful tunes for tomorrow night at Hero's bedroom window.

Balthasar: The best I can find, my lord.

Don Pedro: Do so. Good-bye. [Exit Balthasar.] Come here, Leonato. What did you tell me before—that your niece Beatrice is in love with Signior Benedick?

Claudio: Yes. [Aside to Don Pedro] Continue to stalk, our prey sits. [Louder for Benedick to hear] I didn't think the lady would ever love any man.

Leonato: Nor I, neither. But it is so strange that she has an eye for Signior Benedick, since her outward appearance towards him is so contemptuous.

Benedick: [Aside] Is it possible? Can the wind come from that direction?

Leonato: In truth, my lord, I don't know what to think of it, but she loves him so deeply that I can't imagine it.

Don Pedro: Maybe she is faking her affection.

Claudio: Sure, that's it.

Leonato: God, counterfeiting her love? There was never a deception that came as real as her passion.

73

DON PEDRO: Why, what effects of passion shows she?

CLAUDIO: [aside] Bait the hook well! This fish will bite.

100 LEONATO: What effects, my lord? She will sit you—you heard my daughter tell you how.

CLAUDIO: She did indeed.

DON PEDRO: How, how, I pray you? You amaze me. I would have thought her spirit had been invincible against all assaults of affection.

105 LEONATO: I would have sworn it had, my lord—especially against Benedick.

BENEDICK: [Aside] I should think this a gull but that the white-bearded fellow speaks it. Knavery cannot, sure, hide himself in such reverence.

110 CLAUDIO: [Aside] He hath ta'en th' infection. Hold it up.

DON PEDRO: Hath she made her affection known to Benedick?

LEONATO: No, and swears she never will. That's her torment.

CLAUDIO: 'Tis true indeed. So your daughter says. 'Shall I,' says she, 'that have so oft encountered him with scorn, write to him
115 that I love him?'"

LEONATO: This says she now when she is beginning to write to him; for she'll be up twenty times a night, and there will she sit in her smock till she have writ a sheet of paper. My daughter tells us all.

120 CLAUDIO: Now you talk of a sheet of paper, I remember a pretty jest your daughter told us of.

DON PEDRO: Why, what evidence does she show of passion?

CLAUDIO: [Aside] Bait the hook well! This fish will bite.

LEONATO: What evidence, my lord? She will sit you—you heard my daughter say how.

CLAUDIO: She did indeed.

DON PEDRO: How, How, please tell me? I'm amazed. I thought that she would have never felt love.

LEONATO: I would have sworn it also, my lord—especially against Benedick.

BENEDICK: [Aside] I'd think this to be a trick but the aged man speaks it. Deceptions cannot hide in such years as his.

CLAUDIO: [Aside] He's hooked. Keep going.

DON PEDRO: Has she made known her feelings to Benedick?

LEONATO: No, and she swears she never will. That's her torment.

CLAUDIO: That's true. That's what Hero says. Beatrice says, "How can I write to him telling of my love when I've been so cruel?"

LEONATO: She says this whenever she begins to write. She'll be up 20 times a night in her nightgown, sitting and writing. Hero tells us everything.

CLAUDIO: Now you talk about sheets of paper, I recall a joke that Beatrice told us.

LEONATO: O, when she had writ it, and was reading it over, she found Benedick and Beatrice between the sheet?

CLAUDIO: That.

125 LEONATO: O, she tore the letter into a thousand halfpence, railed at herself that she should be so immodest to write to one that she knew would flout her. 'I measure him,' says she, 'by my own spirit; for I should flout him if he writ to me. Yea, though I love him, I should.'

130 CLAUDIO: Then down upon her knees she falls, weeps, sobs, beats her heart, tears her hair, prays, curses—O sweet Benedick! God give me patience!'

LEONATO: She doth indeed; my daughter says so. And the ecstasy hath so much overborne her that my daughter is sometime 135 afeard she will do a desperate outrage to herself. It is very true.

DON PEDRO: It were good that Benedick knew of it by some other, if she will not discover it.

CLAUDIO: To what end? He would make but a sport of it and tor- 140 ment the poor lady worse.

DON PEDRO: An he should, it were an alms to hang him! She's an excellent sweet lady, and, out of all suspicion, she is virtuous.

CLAUDIO: And she is exceeding wise.

DON PEDRO: In everything but in loving Benedick.

LEONATO: Yes, when she had written it and was reading it over, she found Benedick and Beatrice between the sheets.

CLAUDIO: That's the one.

LEONATO: Oh, how she tore the note into a thousand tiny pieces; she yelled at herself that she should be so forward as to write to someone who rejected her. "I judge him by my own spirit for I would reject him if he wrote to me. I would even though I love him."

CLAUDIO: She then falls on her knees, weeps, sobs, beats her breast, tears her hair, prays, curses "Oh sweet Benedick! God help me."

LEONATO: Indeed she does—so says Hero. And her excess has so much overcome her that Hero fears she may do something desperate. It's very true.

DON PEDRO: It would be good that someone told Benedick if she won't tell him.

CLAUDIO: To what purpose? He would only make fun of her and torment her even worse.

DON PEDRO: If he did, it would be a good deed to hang him! She's such a fine lady, exceedingly virtuous, and free of any suspicion.

CLAUDIO: And she is very wise.

DON PEDRO: In everything except loving Benedick.

145   LEONATO: O, my lord, wisdom and blood combating in so tender a body, we have ten proofs to one that blood hath the victory. I am sorry for her, as I have just cause, being her uncle and her guardian.

DON PEDRO: I would she had bestowed this dotage on me. I would
150   have daffed all other respects and made her half myself. I pray you tell Benedick of it and hear what 'a will say.

LEONATO: Were it good, think you?

CLAUDIO: Hero thinks surely she will die; for she says she will die if he love her not, and she will die ere she make her love
155   known, and she will die, if he woo her, rather than she will bate one breath of her accustomed crossness.

DON PEDRO: She doth well. If she should make tender of her love, 'tis very possible he'll scorn it; for the man, as you know all hath a contemptible spirit.

160   CLAUDIO: He is a very proper man.

DON PEDRO: He hath indeed a good outward happiness.

CLAUDIO: Before God! and in my mind, very wise.

DON PEDRO: He doth indeed show some sparks that are like wit.

CLAUDIO: And I take him to be valiant.

165   DON PEDRO: As Hector, I assure you; and in the managing of quarrels you may say he is wise, for either he avoids them with great discretion, or undertakes them with a most Christianlike fear.

78

LEONATO: *Alas, my lord, when wisdom and passion war in such a tender body, we know that the odds are that passion will win out. I am very sorry for her, since I'm her uncle and guardian.*

DON PEDRO: *I wish she had shown this affection to me. I would have put aside all other loves and made her my better half. I think you should tell Benedick of it and hear what he will say.*

LEONATO: *Do you think it is good to do so?*

CLAUDIO: *Hero thinks that Beatrice will die, for she says she will die if he doesn't love her, and she will die rather than to tell of her love, and she will die if he woos her, rather than she will change her usual harsh nature.*

DON PEDRO: *She does well in not telling him. If she made her love known, it's probable that he would scorn her. For the man has a contemptuous spirit.*

CLAUDIO: *He is a handsome man.*

DON PEDRO: *He does have an attractive appearance.*

CLAUDIO: *Yes, by God! And he is very wise.*

DON PEDRO: *He has some actions which are similar to humor.*

CLAUDIO: *And he is brave.*

DON PEDRO: *Like the Greek hero Hector, he avoids fights with discretion or undertakes a fight with Christianlike fear.*

LEONATO: If he do fear God, 'a must necessarily keep peace. If he
170 break the peace, he ought to enter into a quarrel with fear and
trembling.

DON PEDRO: And so will he do; for the man doth fear God, how-
soever it seems not in him by some large jests he will make.
Well, I am sorry for your niece. Shall we go seek Benedick
175 and tell him of her love?

CLAUDIO: Never tell him, my lord. Let her wear it out with good
counsel.

LEONATO: Nay, that's impossible; she may wear her heart out first.

DON PEDRO: Well, we will hear further of it by your daughter. Let
180 it cool the while. I love Benedick well, and I could wish he
would modestly examine himself to see how much he is
unworthy so good a lady.

LEONATO: My lord, will you walk? Dinner is ready.

[They walk away.]

CLAUDIO: If he do not dote on her upon this, I will never trust my
185 expectation.

DON PEDRO: Let there be the same net spread for her, and that must
your daughter and her gentlewomen carry. The sport will be,
when they hold one an opinion of another's dotage, and no
such matter. That's the scene that I would see, which will be
190 merely a dumb show. Let us send her to call him in to dinner.
[Exeunt Don Pedro, Claudio, and Leonato.]

BENEDICK: This can be no trick. The conference was sadly borne;
they have the truth of this from Hero; they seem to pity the
lady. It seems her affections have their full bent. Love me?

LEONATO: If he fears God, he should keep the peace or fear the consequences.

DON PEDRO: He will, for he does fear God, despite what some of his antics indicate. Well, I am sorry for your niece. Shall we go find Benedick and tell him of Beatrice's love?

CLAUDIO: Never tell him, my lord. Let her get over it with counseling.

LEONATO: No, that's impossible; she'd wear out her heart first.

DON PEDRO: We will discuss this with Hero further. Let it cool the while. I like Benedick a great deal, and I could wish that he would examine himself to see how unworthy he is of such a good lady.

LEONATO: My Lord, will you walk? Dinner is ready.

[They walk away.]

CLAUDIO: If he doesn't fall in love with her after this, I'll never trust my ability.

DON PEDRO: Let the same trap be set for her by your Hero and her female friends. We will have great fun when each thinks the other is in love when it really isn't so. That's the scene I'll be waiting for; it will be a pantomime. Let's send her to call him in to dinner.
                    [Exit Don Pedro, Claudio, and Leonato.]

BENEDICK: This cannot be a trick. The meeting appeared serious; Hero has told them this information. It appears that Beatrice

195 Why, it must be requited. I hear how I am censured. They say I will bear myself proudly if I perceive the love come from her. They say too that she will rather die than give any sign of affection. I did never think to marry. I must not seem proud. Happy are they that hear their detractions and can put them to mending. They say the lady is fair—'tis a truth, I can bear

200 them witness; and virtuous—'tis so, I cannot reprove it; and wise, but for loving me—by my troth, it is no addition to her wit, nor no great argument of her folly, for I will be hor-ribly in love with her. I may chance have some odd quirks and remnants of wit broken on me because I have railed so

205 long against marriage. But doth not the appetite alters? A man loves the meat in his youth that he cannot endure in his age. Shall quips and sentences and these paper bullets of the brain awe a man from the career of his humour? No, the world must be peopled. When I said I would die a bachelor, I did

210 not think I should live till I were married. Here come Beatrice. By this day! she's a fair lady: I do spy some marks of love in her.

[Enter Beatrice.]

BEATRICE: Against my will I am sent to bid You come in to dinner.

BENEDICK: Fair Beatrice, I thank you for your pains.

215 BEATRICE: I took no more pains for those thanks than you take pains to thank me. If it had been painful, I would not have come.

BENEDICK: You take pleasure then in the message?

BEATRICE: Yea, just so much as you may take upon a knife's point,
220 and choke a daw withal. You have no stomach, signior? Fare you well.

[Exit.]

is madly in love with me. Love me? Well, it must be returned. I hear how I am perceived. They say that I will bear myself too proudly if I know of her love. They say, too, that she would rather die than show her love to me. I never thought of marrying. I must not seem proud. People who correct their faults after hearing of them are happy. They say the lady is fair—and that's a truth I can acknowledge; and virtuous, sure, I can't disprove it, and wise—but for loving me. Well, that's it. I will be terribly in love with her. It's possible she may still poke fun of me because I've been such a tyrant against marriage. Doesn't appetite alter? A man loves dishes in his youth that he cannot stand when he is older. Should jokes and jests frighten a man from action he fancies? No, the world must be peopled. When I said I would die a bachelor, I didn't think I would live long enough to be married. Here comes Beatrice. Why, she is a fine woman. I do see some signs of love in her.

[Enter Beatrice.]

BEATRICE: *Against my will, I am sent here to ask you to come in to dinner.*

BENEDICK: *Sweet Beatrice, thank you for your pains.*

BEATRICE: *It wasn't anymore trouble than you took to thank me. If it were trouble, I wouldn't have come.*

BENEDICK: *Then it was pleasurable?*

BEATRICE: *Yes, as much pleasure as you take by taking a knife's point and choking a bird with it. You aren't hungry, sir? Good-bye!* [Exit.]

BENEDICK: Ha! 'Against my will I am sent to bid you come in to dinner.' There's a double meaning in that. 'I took no more pains for those thanks than you took pains to thank me.' That's as much as to say, 'Any pains that I take for you is as easy as thanks.' If I do not take pity of her, I am a villain; if I do not love her, I am a Jew. I will go get her picture.

225

[Exit.]

BENEDICK: *Ha! "Against my will, I am sent here to ask you to come in to dinner." There's a double meaning in that. "It wasn't anymore trouble than you took to thank me." That's like saying "Pains that I take for you are thanks enough for me." If I don't pity her, I'm a villain; if I don't love her, I'm an outcast. I'll go find her picture and gaze upon it.*

[Exit.]

Act III

Scene 1
Leonato's Orchard

[Enter Hero, Margaret, and Ursula.]

HERO: Good Margaret, run thee to the parlour.
     There shalt thou find my cousin Beatrice
     Proposing with the prince and Claudio.
     Whisper her ear and tell her, I and Ursula
5   Walk in the orchard, and our whole discourse
     Is all of her. Say that thou overheard'st us;
     And bid her steal into the pleached bower,
     Where honeysuckles, ripened by the sun,
     Forbid the sun to enter—like favourites,
10   Made proud by princes, that advance their pride
     Against that power that bred it. There will she hide her
     To listen our propose. This is thy office.
     Bear thee well in it and leave us alone.

MARGARET: I'll make her come, I warrant you, presently.

[Exit.]

15 HERO: Now, Ursula, when Beatrice doth come,
     As we do trace this alley up and down,
     Our talk must only be of Benedick.
     When I do name him, let it be thy part
     To praise him more than ever man did merit.

Act III

Scene 1
Leonato's Orchard

[Enter Hero, Margaret, and Ursula.]

HERO: Margaret, hurry to the parlor. You'll find my cousin Beatrice there talking with Don Pedro and Claudio. Whisper in her ear that Ursula and I are walking in the orange grove, and that our whole conversation is of her. Tell her you overheard us, and you advise her to sneak into the thick bushes of honeysuckle, where ripened by the sun, the honeysuckle now forbids the sun to enter—like court favorites who are nurtured by a ruler and then turn on him. There she may hide to hear our conversations. This is your job, do it well; and now leave us.

MARGARET: I'll get her here now; I promise you.

[Exit.]

HERO: Now Ursula, when Beatrice comes, as we walk back and forth down this path our talk must be only about Benedick. When I bring his name up, your part is to praise him profusely—my part will center on how Benedick is madly in love with Beatrice. Like Cupid's arrow, we will nick her.

20   My talk to thee must be how Benedick
      Is sick in love with Beatrice. Of this matter
      Is little Cupid's crafty arrow made,
      That only wounds by hearsay. [Enter Beatrice.]
      For look where Beatrice like a lapwing runs, now begin;
25   Close by the ground, to hear our conference. [Beatrice hides
      in the arbour].

      URSULA: The pleasant'st angling is to see the fish
      Cut with her golden oars the silver stream.
      And greedily devour the treacherous bait.
30   So angle we for Beatrice, who even now
      Is couched in the woodbine coverture.
      Fear you not my part of the dialogue.

      HERO: Then go we near her, that her ear lose nothing
      Of the false sweet bait that we lay for it.
      [They approach the arbour.]
35   No, truly, Ursula, she is too disdainful.
      I know her spirits are as coy and wild
      As haggards of the rock.

      URSULA: But are you sure
      That Benedick loves Beatrice so entirely?

40   HERO: So says the prince, and my new-trothed lord.

      URSULA: And did they bid you tell her of it, madam?

      HERO: They did entreat me to acquaint her of it;
      But I persuaded them, if they loved Benedick,
      To wish him wrestle with affection,
45   And never to let Beatrice know of it.

      URSULA: Why did you so? Doth not the gentleman
      Deserve as full, as fortunate a bed
      As ever Beatrice shall couch upon?

[Beatrice enters and hides behind bushes.] Let's begin; see where Beatrice, like an injured bird, runs close to the ground to hear our words.

URSULA: *The best fishing involves watching the fish tracking the bait and swallowing it. Let's angle towards Beatrice who is hiding in the honeysuckle bushes. Don't worry about my part in this.*

HERO: *Then let's go near her so she won't miss any of the false baits we spread for her. [They approach.] No truly, Ursula, she is too scornful. Her spirit is as wild and untamed as a hawk.*

URSULA: *But are you positive that Benedick loves her completely?*

HERO: *The prince and Claudio say so.*

URSULA: *And did they tell you to reveal it to her?*

HERO: *They asked me to tell her of it. But I persuaded them, if they really cared for Benedick, to advise him to quench his love and never let Beatrice know about it.*

URSULA: *Why did you do that? Doesn't Benedick deserve the physical rewards of marital bliss as good as Beatrice could provide?*

89

HERO: O god of love! I know he doth deserve
50   As much as may be yielded to a man:
          But Nature never framed a woman's heart
          Of prouder stuff than that of Beatrice.
          Disdain and scorn ride sparkling in her eyes,
          Misprizing what they look on; and her wit
55   Values itself so highly, that to her
          All matter else seems weak. She cannot love,
          Nor take no shape nor project of affection,
          She is so self-endeared.

URSULA: Sure I think so;
60   And therefore certainly it were not good
          She knew his love, lest she'll make sport at it.

HERO: Why, you speak truth. I never yet saw man,
          How wise, how noble, young, how rarely featured,
          But she would spell him backward. If fair-faced,
65   She would swear the gentleman should be her sister;
          If black, why, Nature, drawing of an antique,
          Made a foul blot; if tall, a lance ill-headed;
          If low, an agate very vilely cut;
          If speaking, why, a vane blown with all winds;
70   If silent, why, a block moved with none.
          So turns she every man the wrong side out
          And never gives to truth and virtue that
          Which simpleness and merit purchaseth.

URSULA: Sure, sure, such carping is not commendable.

75 HERO: No, not to be so odd, and from all fashions,
          As Beatrice is, cannot be commendable.
          But who dare tell her so? If I should speak,
          She would mock me into air; O, she would laugh me
          Out of myself, press me to death with wit!
80   Therefore let Benedick, like covered fire,
          Consume away in sighs, waste inwardly.
          It were a better death than die with mocks,
          Which is as bad as die with tickling.

HERO: *Sweet Cupid! I know he deserves as much as any man. But nature never gave a woman's heart more pride than that of Beatrice. Scorn and pride sparkle in her eyes, contemptuous of everything they see; and her humor values itself so highly, that nothing else really matters. She can't love, nor give forth any signs of affection since she values herself so much.*

URSULA: *Yes, I think you're right; so certainly it wouldn't be good that she knew of his love since she'd just tease him.*

HERO: *This is true. I never yet saw a man, no matter how wise, noble, young, or good looking that she wouldn't find fault with. If he would be fair-faced, she would swear he should be her sister. If darker, why then nature made a dark blot. If he were well spoken, she would complain he is windy; If he were quiet, then he is like a block of silent wood. Thus, she turns every man inside out, never admitting virtues and sincerity.*

URSULA: *Yes, yes, such fault-finding is not commendable.*

HERO: *No, to be so removed from accepted practice is wrong. But who would dare to tell her? If I would try, she would abuse me mightily. She would laugh at me so much that I would die under the weight of her wit. Therefore, let Benedick consume away in sighs like a covered pot sputtering. It's a better death than to be killed with sarcasm, which is as bad as dying from tickles.*

91

URSULA: Yet tell her of it. Hear what she will say.

85 HERO: No; rather I will go to Benedick
    And counsel him to fight against his passion.
    And truly, I'll devise some honest slanders
    To stain my cousin with. One doth not know
    How much an ill word may empoison liking.

90 URSULA: O, do not do your cousin such a wrong!
    She cannot be so much without true judgment,
    Having so swift and excellent a wit
    As she is prized to have, as to refuse
    So rare a gentleman as Signior Benedick.

95 HERO: He is the only man of Italy,
    Always excepted my dear Claudio.

URSULA: I pray you be not angry with me, madam,
    Speaking my fancy: Signior Benedick,
    For shape, for bearing, argument, and valour,
100   Goes foremost in report through Italy.

HERO: Indeed he hath an excellent good name.

URSULA: His excellence did earn it ere he had it.
    When are you married, madam?

HERO: Why, every day to-morrow! Come, go in.
105   I'll show thee some attires, and have thy counsel
    Which is the best to furnish me tomorrow. [They walk away.]

URSULA: She's limed, I warrant you! We have caught her, madam.

HERO: If it prove so, then loving goes by haps;
    Some Cupid kills with arrows, some with traps.

    [Exeunt Hero and Ursula. Beatrice advances from the arbour.]

URSULA: *Tell her of this. Hear what she'll say.*

HERO: *No, I'd rather go to Benedick and plead with him to fight his passion. I'll devise some mild criticisms to stain my cousin. One doesn't realize how much a nasty comment might dissuade someone from liking another.*

URSULA: *Don't criticize your cousin so! She can't be so poor of judgement—having such a quick and excellent humor—as to refuse such a terrific man as Signior Benedick.*

HERO: *He's the best man in all of Italy—except for my dear Claudio.*

URSULA: *Excuse me, madam, for speaking my mind, but Signior Benedick for body, for bearing, for intelligence, and for courage is foremost in all Italy.*

HERO: *Yes, he has an excellent reputation.*

URSULA: *He had earned his excellence before he had the accolades. When are you to be married, miss?*

HERO: *Why, every day tomorrow! Come, go in with me. I've got some fine clothes to show you and I want your opinion on how to dress tomorrow. [They walk away.]*

URSULA: *She's caught, I guarantee it! We've caught her, miss.*

HERO: *If that's so, then love comes by chance; some people Cupid kills with arrows and some with traps.*

[Exit Hero and Ursula.]

110 BEATRICE: [coming forward.] What fire is in mine ears? Can this be
true?
Stand I condemned for pride and scorn so much?
Contempt, farewell! and maiden pride, adieu!
   No glory lives behind the back of such.
115 And, Benedick, love on; I will requite thee,
   Taming my wild heart to thy loving hand.
If thou dost love, my kindness shall incite thee
   To bind our loves up in a holy band;
For others say thou dost deserve, and I
120 Believe it better than reportingly.

[Exit.]

Scene 2
A Room in Leonato's House

[Enter Don Pedro, Claudio, Benedick, and Leonato.]

DON PEDRO: I do but stay till your marriage be consummate, and
then go I toward Arragon.

CLAUDIO: I'll bring you thither, my lord, if you'll vouchsafe me.

DON PEDRO: Nay, that would be as great a soil in the new gloss of
5   your marriage as to show a child his new coat and forbid him
to wear it. I will only be bold with Benedick for his company;
for, from the crown of his head to the sole of his foot, he is
all mirth. He hath twice or thrice cut Cupid's bowstring, and
the little hangman dare not shoot at him. He hath a heart as
10   sound as a bell; and his tongue is the clapper, for what his
heart thinks, his tongue speaks.

BENEDICK: Gallants, I am not as I have been.

94

BEATRICE: *[Coming forth from her hiding place] How my ears do burn. Is this so? Am I ridiculed for having too much pride and scorn? Good-bye contempt! Maiden's arrogance, farewell! There is no happiness in these things. Benedick, love on; I'll repay you, taming my wild heart to your loving hand. If you love, then my kindness will lead you to bind our hearts in marriage. Others say you deserve it, and I believe it is not merely gossip.*

[Exit.]

Scene 2
A Room in Leonato's House

[Enter Don Pedro, Claudio, Benedick, and Leonato.]

DON PEDRO: *I will stay only until your marriage takes place and then I'm off to Arragon.*

CLAUDIO: *I'll accompany you there, my lord, if you ask me to.*

DON PEDRO: *No, that would be as big a mistake to your marriage as to show a child new clothes and not let him wear them. I'll only ask Benedick for his companionship, for from his head to his toes he is all comedy. He's beaten Cupid at his own game two or three times, and Cupid no longer shoots at him. His heart is as sound as a bell, and his tongue is its clapper. What his heart thinks, his tongue speaks.*

BENEDICK: *Friends, I am not as I have been.*

Leonato: So say I. Methinks you are sadder.

Claudio: I hope he be in love.

15 Don Pedro: Hang him, truant! There's no true drop of blood in him to be truly touched with love. If he be sad, he wants money.

Benedick: I have the toothache.

Don Pedro: Draw it.

20 Benedick: Hang it!

Claudio: You must hang it first and draw it afterwards.

Don Pedro: What? sigh for the toothache?

Leonato: Where is but a humour or a worm.

Benedick: Well, every one can master a grief, but he that has it.

25 Claudio: Yet say I, he is in love.

Don Pedro: There is no appearance of fancy in him, unless it be a fancy that he hath to strange disguises; as to be a Dutchman to-day, a Frenchman to-morrow; or in the shape of two countries at once, as a German from the waist downward, all slops, 30 and a Spaniard from the hip upward, no doublet. Unless he have a fancy to this foolery, as it appears he hath, he is no fool for fancy, as you would have it appear he is.

LEONATO: I agree. I think you are more serious.

CLAUDIO: I hope he's in love.

DON PEDRO: It can't be, scoundrel! There's not a drop of blood in him which can be reached with love. If he's sad, he needs money.

BENEDICK: I've got a toothache. [A sign of love in Elizabethan times.]

DON PEDRO: Remove the bad tooth.

BENEDICK: Hang it!

CLAUDIO: You've got to hang it first and draw it later.

DON PEDRO: What? Do you sigh with a toothache?

LEONATO: Is your body out of sorts or is it caused by a worm?

BENEDICK: Everyone can conquer pain, except the one who has it.

CLAUDIO: I really think he is in love.

DON PEDRO: There's no sign unless it's this sign of strange clothes. He's dressed like a Dutchman today, maybe a Frenchman tomorrow or really a combination of two styles; he's dressed as a German from his waist down with sloppy pants, and a Spaniard from his waist up with no vest. He is having fun with his clothes since he can't be in love as these garments would suggest.

CLAUDIO: If he be not in love with some woman, there is no
believing old signs. A' brushes his hat o' mornings. What
35   should that bode?

DON PEDRO: Hath any man seen him at the barber's?

CLAUDIO: No, but the barber's man hath been seen with him, and
the old ornament of his cheek hath already stuffed tennis
balls.

40   LEONATO: Indeed he looks younger than he did, by the loss of a
beard.

DON PEDRO: Nay, a' rubs himself with civet. Can you smell him out
by that?

CLAUDIO: That's as much as to say, the sweet youth's in love.

45   DON PEDRO: The greatest note of it is his melancholy.

CLAUDIO: And when was he wont to wash his face?

DON PEDRO: Yea, or to paint himself? for the which I hear what they
say of him.

DON PEDRO: Indeed that tells a heavy tale for him. Conclude,
50   conclude, he is in love.

CLAUDIO: Nay, but I know who loves him.

DON PEDRO: That would I know too. I warrant, one that knows him
not.

CLAUDIO: Yes, and his ill conditions; and in despite of all, dies for
55   him.

CLAUDIO: If he's not in love with a woman, you can't believe old signs. He even brushed his hat this morning—what does that mean?

DON PEDRO: Has anyone seen him at the barber's?

CLAUDIO: No, but the barber's been seen with him, and his old whiskers are already stuffed into tennis balls.

LEONATO: Yes, he does look younger than he did because he shaved off his beard.

DON PEDRO: And he puts on perfume. Can you smell him out by that?

CLAUDIO: That's the same as saying the boy is in love.

DON PEDRO: The biggest giveaway is his melancholic disposition.

CLAUDIO: And when did you ever see him wash his face?

DON PEDRO: Yes, or put on cosmetics like I've heard people say he now does.

DON PEDRO: It looks bad for him. Indeed, indeed, he is in love.

CLAUDIO: No, but I know who loves him.

DON PEDRO: I would like to know that answer too, but I'll bet it is someone who doesn't know him.

CLAUDIO: Yes, and his sorry state. And in despite of everything, she dies for him.

DON PEDRO: She shall be buried with her face upwards.

BENEDICK: Yet is this no charm for the toothache. Old signior, walk aside with me. I have studied eight or nine wise words to speak to you, which these hobby-horses must not hear.

[Exeunt Benedick and Leonato.]

60   DON PEDRO: For my life, to break with him about Beatrice!

CLAUDIO: 'Tis even so. Hero and Margaret have by this played their parts with Beatrice, and then the two bears will not bite one another when they meet.

[Enter Don John the Bastard.]

DON JOHN: My lord and brother, God save you.

65   DON PEDRO: Good den, brother.

DON JOHN: If your leisure served, I would speak with you.

DON PEDRO: In private?

DON JOHN: If it please you. Yet Count Claudio may hear, for what I would speak of concerns him.

70   DON PEDRO: What's the matter?

DON JOHN: [To Claudio] Means your lordship to be married tomorrow?

DON PEDRO: You know he does.

DON JOHN: I know not that, when he knows what I know.

Don Pedro: She'll be buried face upwards.

Benedick: Stop! This won't cure a toothache. [To Leonato] Old gentleman, walk beside me. I've studied some wise words to discuss with you which these buffoons must not hear.

[Exit Benedick and Leonato.]

Don Pedro: I'll bet he's going to discuss Beatrice with Leonato!

Claudio: Sure, that's right. By now Hero and Margaret have played with Beatrice and when those two bears meet, they will not bite one another.

[Enter Don John the Bastard.]

Don John: My brother and my lord, God save you.

Don Pedro: Good evening, brother.

Don John: If you have the time, I'd like to speak to you.

Don Pedro: In private?

Don John: If you wish. But Claudio may hear what I have to say since it concerns him.

Don Pedro: What's the matter?

Don John: [To Claudio] Do you mean to be married tomorrow?

Don Pedro: You know he does.

Don John: I don't know that he will, once he knows what I know.

75 CLAUDIO: If there be any impediment, I pray you discover it.

DON JOHN: You may think I love you not. Let that appear hereaf-
ter, and aim better at me by that I now will manifest. For my
brother, I think he holds you well and in dearness of heart
hath holp to effect your ensuing marriage—surely suit ill
80   spent and labour ill bestowed!

DON PEDRO: Why, what's the matter?

DON JOHN: I came hither to tell you; and, circumstances shortened,
for she has been too long atalking of, the lady is disloyal.

CLAUDIO: Who? Hero?

85 DON JOHN: Even she—Leonato's Hero, your Hero, every man's Hero.

CLAUDIO: Disloyal?

DON JOHN: The word is too good to paint out her wickedness. I
could say she were worse; think you of a worse title, and
I will fit her to it. Wonder not till further warrant. Go but
90   with me to-night, you shall see her chamber window ent'red,
even the night before her wedding day. If you love her then,
to-morrow wed her. But it would better fit your honour to
change your mind.

CLAUDIO: May this be so?

95 DON PEDRO: I will not think it.

DON JOHN: If you dare not trust that you see, confess not that
you know. If you will follow me, I will show you enough;
and when you have seen more and heard more, proceed
accordingly.

CLAUDIO: *If there's any problem, please tell me.*

DON JOHN: *You might not think I like you, but consider that later so you may concentrate on what I will now tell you. I think my brother likes you a great deal and has aided in your proposed marriage—a labor that was ill spent.*

DON PEDRO: *Why? What's the matter?*

DON JOHN: *I came to tell you, and I'll explain quickly—since we've talked too long about her—that the lady is disloyal.*

CLAUDIO: *Who? Hero?*

DON JOHN: *Even she—Leonato's Hero—your Hero—every man's Hero.*

CLAUDIO: *Unfaithful?*

DON JOHN: *The word is too good for her. I'll give it a worse name if you supply the title. Don't doubt it until you hear the particulars. Come with me tonight and see her bedroom entered the night before her wedding day. If you still love her, then marry her tomorrow. But it would be better for your honor to change your mind on this marriage.*

CLAUDIO: *Could this be true?*

DON PEDRO: *I can't believe it.*

DON JOHN: *If you don't believe your eyes, then don't admit what you know. Follow me and I'll show you proof, and then when you've seen it, proceed accordingly.*

100 CLAUDIO: If I see anything to-night why I should not marry her tomorrow, in the congregation where I should wed, there will I shame her.

DON PEDRO: And, as I wooed for thee to obtain her, I will join with thee to disgrace her.

105 DON JOHN: I will disparage her no farther till you are my witnesses. Bear it coldly but till midnight, and let the issue show itself.

DON PEDRO: O day untowardly turned!

CLAUDIO: O mischief strangely thwarting!

110 DON JOHN: O plague right well prevented! So will you say when you have seen the sequel.

[Exeunt.]

Scene 3
A Street

[Enter Dogberry with Verges and the Watch.]

DOGBERRY: Are you good men and true?

VERGES: Yea, or else it were pity but they should suffer salvation, body and soul.

5 DOGBERRY: Nay, that were a punishment too good for them, if they should have any allegiance in them, being chosen for the prince's watch.

CLAUDIO: *If I see any reason tonight as to why I shouldn't marry, then tomorrow in that spot where I was to wed her, I'll shame her in front of everyone.*

DON PEDRO: *And, as I got you into this engagement, I'll help you to disgrace her.*

DON JOHN: *I won't say anything bad about her until you've seen it. Keep quiet until midnight, and let the actions speak for themselves.*

DON PEDRO: *Oh, what an unlucky day!*

CLAUDIO: *Oh, what mischief strangely thwarting this day!*

DON JOHN: *Oh, what an evil prevented! That's what you'll say when you see the unfortunate scene which follows.*

[Exit]

Scene 3
A Street

[Enter Dogberry with Verges and the Watch.]

DOGBERRY: *Are you all good and honest men?*

VERGES: *Yes, or else it would be a pity that they should suffer eternal salvation¹ for it.*

DOGBERRY: *Ah, that would be too good a punishment for the likes of them, being chosen for the prince's guard.*

1. salvation - either Verges means eternal damnation, or Dogberry believes that he did.

VERGES: Well, give them their charge, neighbour Dogberry.

DOGBERRY: First, who think you the most desartless man to be constable?

10   FIRST WATCHMAN: Hugh Oatcake, my lord, or George Seacoal; for they can write and read.

DOGBERRY: Come hither, neighbour Seacoal. God hath blessed you with a good name. To be a well-favoured man is the gift of fortune, but to write and read comes by nature.

15   SECOND WATCHMAN: Both which, Master Constable—

DOGBERRY: You have. I knew it would be your answer. Well, for your favour, my lord, why, give God thanks and make no boast of it; and for your writing and reading, let that appear when there is no need of such vanity. You are thought here
20   to be the most senseless and fit man for the constable of the watch. Therefore bear you the lanthorn. This is your charge: you shall comprehend all vagrom men; you are to bid any man stand, in the prince's name.

SECOND WATCHMAN: How if 'a will not stand?

25   DOGBERRY: Why then, take no note of him, but let him go, and presently call the rest of the watch together and thank God you are rid of a knave.

VERGES: If he will not stand when he is bidden, he is none of the prince's subjects.

VERGES: *Give them their instructions, neighbor Dogberry.*

DOGBERRY: *First, who do you think is the most desartless² man to be in charge?*

FIRST WATCHMAN: *Hugh Oatcake, sir, or George Seacole, since they both can read and write.*

DOGBERRY: *Come here, neighbor Seacole. God has blessed you with a fine name. To be a good-looking man is pure luck, but to read and write comes by nature.*

SECOND WATCHMAN: *Both of which, master constable—*

DOGBERRY: *You have. I knew that would be your answer. Well, for your appearance, sir, give God thanks and make no boast about it; and as for your reading and writing, let them be noticed when there is no need of such vanity. You are thought to be the most senseless³ and fit man to be in charge of the watch. Therefore, take this lantern. This is your duty! You shall comprehend⁴ all vagrom⁵ men; you are to tell any man to stop in the name of the prince.*

SECOND WATCHMAN: *What if he won't stop?*

DOGBERRY: *Why then, ignore him. Let him go and call the rest of the watch together and thank God you are rid of a villain.*

VERGES: *If he will not stop when asked to, he is not one of the prince's subjects.*

2. desartless - Dogberry's weak grasp of vocabulary causes him to choose an inappropriate, and therefore, comic word instead of the word he wanted. Here, he was trying to say 'desirable.'
3. senseless - sensible
4. comprehend - apprehend
5. vagrom - vagrant

107

30   DOGBERRY: True, and they are to meddle with none but the prince's
subjects. You shall also make no noise in the streets; for for
the watch to babble and to talk is most tolerable, and not to
be endured.

SECOND WATCHMAN: We will rather sleep than talk. We know what
35   belongs to a watch.

DOGBERRY: Why, you speak like an ancient and most quiet watchman, for I cannot see how sleeping should offend. Only have
a care that your bills be not stolen. Well, you are to call at all
the alehouses and bid those that are drunk get them to bed.

40   SECOND WATCHMAN: How if they will not?

DOGBERRY: Why then, let them alone till they are sober. If they
make you not then the better answer, you may say they are
not the men you took them for.

SECOND WATCHMAN: Well, my lord.

45   DOGBERRY: If you meet a thief, you may suspect him, by virtue of
your office, to be no true man; and for such kind of men, the
less you meddle or make with them, why, the more is for your
honesty.

SECOND WATCHMAN: If we know him to be a thief, shall we not lay
50   hands on him?

DOGBERRY: Truly, by your office you may; but I think they that
touch pitch will be defiled. The most peaceable way for you, if
you do take a thief, is to let him show himself what he is, and
steal out of your company.

Dogberry: True, and you are to meddle with only the prince's sub-
    jects. You should be quiet in the streets, for you to gossip and
    talk is most tolerable[6] and should not be endured.

Second Watchman: We would rather sleep than talk. We know
    how our job works.

Dogberry: You speak like an old and quiet watchman, for I can't
    see how sleeping should disturb anyone. Only be careful that
    your weapons aren't stolen. Further, you are to stop at the
    taverns and ask the drunks to go to bed.

Second Watchman: What if they won't go home to bed?

Dogberry: Then let them alone until they become sober. If they
    can't give you a good answer then, you can say they were not
    the men you thought they were.

Second Watchman: Good, my lord.

Dogberry: Further, if you meet a thief, you may suspect him by
    your duty not to be an honest man; and with that kind the less
    you deal with them the better will be your honesty.

Second Watchman: If we know him to be a thief, shouldn't we
    grab him?

Dogberry: Indeed you may by your duty, but I think that those who
    handle tar will become dirty. The easiest thing for you to do if
    you seize a thief is to let him show his true nature by stealing
    out of your company.

6.   tolerable - intolerable

55   VERGES: You have been always called a merciful man, partner.

DOGBERRY: Truly, I would not hang a dog by my will, much more a man who hath any honesty in him.

VERGES: If you hear a child cry in the night, you must call to the nurse and bid her still it.

60   SECOND WATCH: How if the nurse be asleep and will not hear us?

DOGBERRY: Why then, depart in peace and let the child wake her with crying; for the ewe that will not hear her lamb when it baes will never answer a calf when he bleats.

VERGES: 'Tis very true.

65   DOGBERRY: This is the end of the charge—you, constable, are to present the prince's own person: if you meet the prince in the night, you may stay him.

VERGES: Nay, by'r lady, that I think 'a cannot.

DOGBERRY: Five shillings to one on't with any man that knows the
70   statutes, he may stay him! Marry, not without the prince be willing; for indeed the watch ought to offend no man, and it is an offence to stay a man against his will.

VERGES: By'r lady, I think it be so.

DOGBERRY: Ha, ah, ha! Well, masters, good night. An there be any
75   matter of weight chances, call up me. Keep your fellows' counsels and your own, and good night. Come, neighbour.

VERGES: *You've always been called a merciful man, partner.*

DOGBERRY: *Yes, I would not hang a dog much less a man, who has any honesty in him.*

VERGES: *If you hear a baby crying in the night, you must call the nurse and have her still the child.*

SECOND WATCHMAN: *What if the nurse be asleep and cannot hear us?*

DOGBERRY: *Then leave in peace and let the child's crying wake her; for the female sheep who will not hear her lamb when it baes will never answer a calf when he bleats.*

VERGES: *That's so true.*

DOGBERRY: *This is the end of your instructions: constable, you are to present⁷ even the prince; if you meet him in the night, you must stop him.*

VERGES: *By our lady, I don't think I can do that.*

DOGBERRY: *Five to one bet on it: any man can stop him that knows the laws. But, not without the prince's approval; since the watch should offend no man, and it is against the law to hold someone against their will.*

VERGES: *By your lady, I think that's right.*

DOGBERRY: *Well, gentlemen, good night. If there's a big problem, wake me. Help each other out and good night. Come friend.*

---

7.   present - detain; prevent him from continuing

SECOND WATCHMAN: Well, masters, we hear our charge. Let us go sit here upon the church bench till two, and then all to bed.

DOGBERRY: One word more, honest neighbours. I pray you watch
80   about Signior Leonato's door; for the wedding being there tomorrow, there is a great coil to-night. Adieu. Be vigitant, I beseech you

        [Exeunt Dogberry, Verges, Borachio and Conrade.]

BORACHIO: What, Conrade!

SECOND WATCHMAN: [aside] Peace! stir not!

85   BORACHIO: Conrade, I say!

CONRADE: Here, man. I am at thy elbow.

BORACHIO: Mass, and my elbow itched! I thought there would a scab follow.

CONRADE: I will owe thee an answer for that; and now forward with
90   thy tale.

BORACHIO: Stand thee close then under this penthouse, for it drizzles rain, and I will, like a true drunkard, utter all to thee.

SECOND WATCHMAN: [Aside] Some treason, masters. Yet stand close.

BORACHIO: Therefore know I have earned of Don John a thousand
95   ducats.

CONRADE: Is it possible that any villany should be so dear?

SECOND WATCHMAN: *Well, men, we hear our orders. Let's go sit in front of the church until two, and then we can go to bed.*

DOGBERRY: *One more thing, friends. Please watch outside Signior Leonato's home; for there is to be a wedding tomorrow and tonight will be wild. Be vigitant,*⁸ *I implore you.*

[Exit Dogberry and Verges. Enter Borachio and Conrade.]

BORACHIO: *Ho, Conrade!*

SECOND WATCHMAN: *Shhh. Quiet!*

BORACHIO: *Conrade, I say!*

CONRADE: *Here, man. I'm at your elbow.*

BORACHIO: *By the church, and my elbow itched. I thought a scab would follow.*

CONRADE: *I'll get you for that, but first tell me your story.*

BORACHIO: *It's drizzling; come over here under the eaves, and I will tell you everything.*

SECOND WATCHMAN: *[Aside] Some treason is afoot, friends. Come closer.*
BORACHIO: *Know you that I earned 1,000 gold coins from Don John.*

CONRADE: *Is it possible for any villainous work to be so expensive?*

8.   vigitant - vigilant

BORACHIO: Thou shouldst rather ask if it were possible any villany should not be so rich; for when rich villains have need of poor ones, poor ones may make what price they will.

100   CONRADE: I wonder at it.

BORACHIO: That shows thou art unconfirmed. Thou knowest that the fashion of a doublet, or a hat, or a cloak, is nothing to a man.

[Several obscure lines regarding fashion and male sexuality are deleted here.]

CONRADE: All this I see; and I see that the fashion wears out more
105   apparel than the man. But art not thou thyself giddy with the fashion too, that thou hast shifted out of thy tale into telling me of the fashion?

BORACHIO: Not so neither. But know that I have to-night wooed Margaret, the Lady Hero's gentlewoman, by the name of Hero.
110   She leans me out at her mistress' chamber window, bids me a thousand times good night—I tell this tale vilely; I should first tell thee how the prince, Claudio and my master, planted and placed and possessed by my master Don John, saw afar off in the orchard this amiable encounter.

115   CONRADE: And thought they Margaret was Hero?

BORACHIO: Two of them did, the prince and Claudio; but the devil my master knew she was Margaret; and partly by his oaths, which first possessed them, partly by the dark night, which did deceive them, but chiefly by my villany, which did con-
120   firm any slander that Don John had made, away went Claudio enraged; swore he would meet her, as he was appointed, next morning at the temple, and there, before the whole congre-gation, shame her with what he saw o'ernight and send her home again without a husband.

BORACHIO: *You should ask if it is possible for any evil work not to be so costly. For when rich villains need poor villains, then poor villains may set whatever price they want.*

CONRADE: *I'm amazed.*

BORACHIO: *That shows you are not knowledgeable.*

[Several obscure lines regarding fashion and male sexuality are deleted here.]

CONRADE: *I see this and I also see that fashion wears out clothing faster than a man can. But are you not giddy with this fashion business? You have shifted from telling me the tale and are lecturing me on fashion.*

BORACHIO: *Neither one of those is so. But, know you that tonight I have wooed Margaret, Hero's servant, calling her by the name of Hero. As I do, she leans out of Hero's bedroom window, bidding me good night a thousand times—but I tell this tale poorly. I need to first tell you how the prince and Claudio were led to a hiding spot in the orchard by Don John, and from afar the three saw this lovers' encounter.*

CONRADE: *And they thought Margaret was Hero?*

BORACHIO: *Two of them did, the prince and Claudio. But that devil, my master, knew she was really Margaret. Partly by his lies which he first told them, and partly by the darkness of night which did deceive them—but mainly by my villainy which confirmed all which Don John had spoken—Claudio left enraged; he swore he would meet her at church tomorrow morning and humiliate her in front of all those gathered and send her home without a husband.*

125   FIRST WATCHMAN: We charge you in the prince's name stand!

SECOND WATCHMAN: Call up the right master constable. We have here recovered the most dangerous piece of lechery that ever was known in the commonwealth.

FIRST WATCHMAN: And one Deformed is one of them. I know him; a' 130   wears a lock.

CONRADE: Masters, masters—

SECOND WATCHMAN: You'll be made bring Deformed forth, I warrant you.

CONRADE: Masters—

135   SECOND WATCHMAN: Never speak; we charge you, let us obey you to go with us.

BORACHIO: We are like to prove a goodly commodity, being taken up of these men's bills.

CONRADE: A commodity in question, I warrant you. Come, we'll 140   obey you.

[Exeunt.]

FIRST WATCHMAN: *Stop in the name of the prince!*

SECOND WATCHMAN: *Call up Constable Dogberry. We have recovered[9] the most awful crime of lechery[10] that ever happened in this country.*

FIRST WATCHMAN: *And one whose name is Deformed is one of the offenders. I know him by his hair style.*

CONRADE: *Friends, friends—*

FIRST WATCHMAN: *You'll pay for this, Deformed, count on it.*

CONRADE: *Friends—*

SECOND WATCHMAN: *Shut up, that's an order. You better obey and go with us.*

BORACHIO: *We are likely to be good merchandise stopped by these men's weapons.*

CONRADE: *Questionable merchandise if you ask me. Come, we'll obey you.*

[All Exit.]

9. recovered - uncovered
10. lechery - treachery

Scene 4
A Room in Leonato's House

[Enter Hero, Margaret and Ursula.]

HERO: Good Ursula, wake my cousin Beatrice and desire her to rise.

URSULA: I will, lady.

HERO: And bid her come hither.

URSULA: Well.   [Exit.]

5   MARGARET: Troth, I think your other rebato were better.

HERO: No, pray thee, good Meg, I'll wear this.

MARGARET: By my troth, is not so good; and I warrant your cousin
          will say so.

HERO: My cousin 's a fool, and thou art another. I'll wear none but
10   this.

MARGARET: I like the new tire within excellently, if the hair were
          a thought browner; and your gown's a most rare fashion, i'
          faith. I saw the Duchess of Milan's gown that they praise so.

HERO: O, that exceeds, they say.

15   MARGARET: By my troth's but a nightgown in respect of yours—
          cloth-o'-gold and cuts, and laced with silver, set with pearls
          down sleeves, side-sleeves, and skirts, round underborne with
          a blush tinsel. But for a fine, quaint, graceful, and excellent
          fashion, yours is worth ten on't.

Scene 4
A Room in Leonato's House

[Enter Hero, Margaret and Ursula.]

HERO: Good Ursula, wake Beatrice and tell her to get up.

URSULA: Yes, lady.

HERO: Have her come here.

URSULA: Yes.   [Exit.]

MARGARET: In truth, I like your other collar better.

HERO: No, Meg, I'll wear this one.

MARGARET: I honestly don't think it's very nice, and Beatrice will agree.

HERO: My cousin is a fool and so are you. I'll wear none but this one.

MARGARET: I like the new one in the other room more; it goes with your hair better and also your gown. I saw the Duchess of Milan's gown that everyone is talking about.

HERO: They say it's too gaudy.

MARGARET: Oh, it's only a nightshirt in comparison to yours—with its gold and pleats laced with silver, set with pearls down the sleeves, and the extra sleeves and skirts with all the ornamentation underneath. But for a fine and elegant dress, yours is worth ten like it.

20   Hero: God give me joy to wear it! for my heart is exceeding heavy.

Margaret: 'Twill be heavier soon by the weight of a man.

Hero: Fie upon thee! art not ashamed?

Margaret: Of what, lady? of speaking honourably? Is not marriage honourable in a beggar? Is not your lord honourable without
25   marriage? I think you would have me say, 'saving your reverence, a husband.' An bad thinking do not wrest true speaking, I'll offend nobody. Is there any harm in 'the heavier for a husband'? None, I think, an it be the right husband and the right wife. Otherwise 'tis light, and not heavy. Ask my Lady
30   Beatrice else. Here she comes.

[Enter Beatrice.]

Hero: Good morrow, coz.

Beatrice: Good morrow, sweet Hero.

Hero: Why, how now? Do you speak in the sick tune?

Beatrice: I am out of all other tune, methinks.

35   Margaret: Clap's into 'Light o' love.' That goes without a burden. Do you sing it, and I'll dance it.

Beatrice: Ye, 'Light o' love' with your heels! then, if your husband have stables enough, you'll see he shall lack no barns.

Margaret: O illegitimate construction! I scorn that with my heels.

Beatrice: 'Tis almost five o'clock, cousin; 'tis time you were ready.
40   By my troth, I am exceeding ill. Heigh-ho!

HERO: *God give me joy to wear it, for my heart is really heavy.*

MARGARET: *It'll be heavier soon by the weight of a man.*

HERO: *Shame on you—are you not embarrassed?*

MARGARET: *Of what? Of speaking honorably? Isn't marriage honorable even with a beggar? Isn't Claudio honorable even without marriage? I think you want me to say "Excuse me, I meant weight of a husband." If poor thinking can't twist accurate judgement, I won't offend. Is it wrong to say "the heavier for a husband?" Not at all between husband and wife. Otherwise would be wrong. Ask Beatrice. Here she comes.*

[Enter Beatrice.]

HERO: *Morning, coz.*

BEATRICE: *Morning, Hero.*

HERO: *What? Do you sing in a sickly tune?*

BEATRICE: *I'm out of all tunes, I think.*

MARGARET: *Sing "Light of Love." That's easy enough. You sing, and I'll dance it.*

BEATRICE: *You're always falling lightly for men. If your husband has room, you'll see that he has many children.*

MARGARET: *Shameful! I think I'll leave.*

BEATRICE: *It's almost five o'clock cousin; time to get you ready. Gosh, I'm sick.*

MARGARET: For a hawk, a horse, or a husband?

BEATRICE: For the letter that begins them all, H.

MARGARET: Well, an you be not turned Turk, there's no more sailing by the star.

45 BEATRICE: What means the fool, trow?

MARGARET: Nothing I; but God send every one their heart's demy lorde!

HERO: These gloves the count sent me, they are an excellent perfume.

50 BEATRICE: I am stuffed, cousin; I cannot smell.

MARGARET: A maid, and stuffed! There's goodly catching of cold.

BEATRICE: O, God help me! God help me! How long have you professed apprehension?

55 MARGARET: Ever since you left it. Doth not my wit become me rarely?

BEATRICE: It is not seen enough. You should wear it in your cap. By my troth, I am sick.

MARGARET: Get you some of this distilled Carduus Benedictus and lay it on your heart. It is the only thing for a qualm.

60 HERO: There thou prickest her with a thistle.

BEATRICE: Benedictus? Why Benedictus? You have some moral in this Benedictus?

MARGARET: *For a hawk, a horse, or a husband?*

BEATRICE: *For the letter that starts them all, "H."*

MARGARET: *If you haven't turned pagan, there's no more sailing by the navigating star.*

BEATRICE: *What does this fool mean?*

MARGARET: *I don't mean anything, except that God sends everyone their heart's desire.*

HERO: *These gloves that the count sent me smell of a wonderful perfume.*

BEATRICE: *I can't smell anything, My nose is stuffed.*

MARGARET: *A young lady and pregnant! You really caught something with your cold.*

BEATRICE: *God help me. How long have you pretended to be funny?*

MARGARET: *Ever since you stopped. Don't I have a rare humor?*

BEATRICE: *[sarcastically]   Yes, it's not seen often enough. You should show it off more. But, really, I am sick.*

MARGARET: *Then get some Carduus Benedictus [holy herb] and lay it next to your heart. It's the only thing for your pain.*

HERO: *You wound her with this thistle.*

BEATRICE: *Benedictus? Why that? Have you a double meaning in this Benedictus?*

MARGARET: Moral? No, by my troth, I have no moral meaning; I
meant, plain holy thistle. You may think perchance that I
65 think you are in love. Nay, by'r lady, I am not such a fool to
think what I list; nor I list not to think what I can; nor indeed
I cannot think, if I would think my heart out of thinking,
that you are in love, or that you will be in love, or that you
can be in love. Yet Benedick was such another, and now is he
70 become a man. He swore he would never marry; and yet now,
in despite of his heart, he eats his meat without grudging; and
how you may be converted I know not, but methinks you
look with your eyes as other women do.

BEATRICE: What pace is this that thy tongue keeps?

75 MARGARET: Not a false gallop.

URSULA: Madam, withdraw. The prince, the count, Signior
Benedick, Don John, and all the gallants of the town are come
to fetch you to church.

HERO: Help to dress me, good coz, good Meg, good Ursula.

Scene 5
Another Room in Leonato's House

[Enter Leonato, Constable Dogberry and Headborough Verges.]

LEONATO: What would you with me, honest neighbour?

DOGBERRY: Marry, my lord, I would have some confidence with you
that decerns you nearly.

MARGARET: Double meaning? Honestly, not me. I meant only the herb. You may think that I think you are in love. No, I'm not foolish enough to think what I please, nor pleased to think what I may. I can't think since if I thought with my heart, I'd be thinking you're in love, or would be in love, or could be in love. And Benedick is also like you and has now become a normal man. He swore he would never marry but now, despite his heart, he doesn't complain about his meals. I don't know how you have changed, but I think you now look with eyes as other women do.

BEATRICE: What a fast pace your tongue makes.

MARGARET: Not a fake pace.

URSULA: Madam, go inside! The prince, the count, Benedick, Don John and all the nobility of the town have come to escort you to church.

HERO: Beatrice, Meg, Ursula, help me dress.

Scene 5
Another Room in Leonato's House

[Enter Leonato, Constable Dogberry and Headborough Verges.]

LEONATO: Neighbor, what do you want?

DOGBERRY: Well, my lord, I need to have a confidence[1] with you that decerns[2] you.

1. confidence - conference
2. decerns - concerns

LEONATO: Brief, I pray you; for you see it is a busy time with me.

5   DOGBERRY: Marry, this it is, my lord.

VERGES: Yes, in truth it is, my lord.

LEONATO: What is it, my good friends?

DOGBERRY: Goodman Verges, my lord, speaks a little off the matter—an old man, my lord, and his wits are not so blunt as,
10   God help, I would desire they were; but, in faith, honest as
the skin between his brows.

VERGES: Yes, I thank God I am as honest as any man living that is
an old man and no honester than I.

DOGBERRY: Comparisons are odorous. Palabras, neighbour Verges.

15   LEONATO: Neighbours, you are tedious.

DOGBERRY: It pleases your worship to say so, but we are the poor
Duke's officers; but truly, for mine own part, if I were as
tedious as a king, I could find in my heart to bestow it all of
your worship.

20   LEONATO: All thy tediousness on me, ah?

DOGBERRY: Yea, in 'twere a thousand pound more than 'tis; for I
hear as good exclamation on your worship as of any man in
the city; and though I be but a poor man, I am glad to hear it.

126

LEONATO: *Please, be brief. You can see it's a busy time for me.*

DOGBERRY: *Indeed it is, my lord.*

VERGES: *Yes, indeed it is, my lord.*

LEONATO: *Well, what is it, my friends?*

DOGBERRY: *Verges, here, speaks a little off the matter—he's an old man, sir, and his brain is not as blunt³ as I'd like it; but he, in truth, is as honest as the skin on his forehead.*

VERGES: *Yes, thank God, I'm as honest as any man my age who's still living and isn't more honest than I am.*

DOGBERRY: *Comparisons are odorous⁴. Be brief, Verges.*

LEONATO: *Friends, you are tedious⁵.*

DOGBERRY: *Thanks so much for saying so, but we remain the humble Duke's officers. Really though, if I was as tedious as a king, I could give it all to you, sir.*

LEONATO: *All your tedious nature to me?*

DOGBERRY: *Yes, even if it were a thousand pounds more than it is, for I hear great exclamation⁶ about you as any man in the city. Though I am poor, I still am glad to hear it.*

3. blunt - sharp
4. odorous - odious
5. tedious - in this instance, Dogberry, unaware that 'tedious' means boring, assumes he is being complimented by Leonato.
6. exclamation - acclamation

VERGES: And so am I.

25 LEONATO: I would fain know what you have to say.

VERGES: Marry, my lord, our watch to-night, excepting your worship's presence, ha' ta'en a couple of as arrant knaves as any in
Messina.

DOGBERRY: A good old man, my lord; he will be talking. As they say,
30 'When the age is in, the wit is out.' God help us! it is a world
to see! Well said, i' faith, neighbour Verges. Well, God's a
good man. An two men ride of a horse, one must ride behind.
An honest soul, i' faith, my lord, by my troth he is, as ever
broke bread; but God is to be worshipped; all men are not
35 alike, alas, good neighbour!

LEONATO: Indeed, neighbour, he comes too short of you.

DOGBERRY: Gifts that God gives.

LEONATO: I must leave you.

DOGBERRY: One word, my lord. Our watch, my lord, have indeed
40 comprehended two aspicious persons, and we would have
them this morning examined before your worship.

LEONATO: Take their examination yourself and bring it me. I am
now in great haste, as it may appear unto you.

DOGBERRY: It shall be suffigance.

45 LEONATO: Drink some wine ere you go. Fare you well.

loves company, speaks her mind, sings, plays, and dances well. Where there are impressive qualities, these are more praiseworthy. Nor will I worry about her leaving me, for my lack of self-worth, because she had eyes, and she chose me. No, Iago, I will see, before I doubt. When I doubt, I will look for proof, and if there is proof, then that is that. To hell with love or jealousy!

IAGO: I am glad to hear it, because now I have a reason to show the love and duty that I have for you with an open spirit. Therefore, because I am so devoted to you, take this from me. I do not have proof. Watch your wife; observe her with Cassio. Do not be jealous or unsuspecting either; I would not like to see your free and noble nature, abused because of your own generosity. Watch them. I know what people from Venice are like; they let heaven see the deeds that they do not dare show their husbands. Their way of living is to commit the deed, but keep it secret.

OTHELLO: You think so?

IAGO: Desdemona deceived her father to marry you. When she pretended to fear you, she actually loved you.

OTHELLO: Yes, she did.

IAGO: Why, it's obvious. She, so young, could act well enough to keep her father blind—he thought it was witchcraft. I deserve a lot of the blame; I humbly ask you to excuse me for loving you too much.

He thought 'twas witchcraft—but I am much to blame;
I humbly do beseech you of your pardon
For too much loving you.

OTHELLO: I am bound to thee forever.

240   IAGO: I see this hath a little dash'd your spirits.

OTHELLO: Not a jot, not a jot.

IAGO: I'faith, I fear it has.
      I hope you will consider what is spoke
      Comes from my love. But I do see you're moved;
245   I am to pray you not to strain my speech
      To grosser issues, nor to larger reach
      Than to suspicion.

OTHELLO: I will not.

IAGO: Should you do so, my lord,
250   My speech should fall into such vile success
      Which my thoughts aim not at. Cassio's my worthy friend—
      My lord, I see you're moved.

OTHELLO: No, not much moved.
      I do not think but Desdemona's honest.

255   IAGO: Long live she so! and long live you to think so!

OTHELLO: And yet, how nature erring from itself—

IAGO: Ay, there's the point, as—to be bold with you—
      Not to affect many proposed matches
      Of her own clime, complexion, and degree,
260   Whereto we see in all things nature tends—
      Foh, one may smell in such a will most rank,

OTHELLO: I am bound to you forever.

IAGO: I see this has upset you a bit.

OTHELLO: Not at all, not at all.

IAGO: Honestly, I am afraid it has. I hope you will remember that the things I have said come from my love for you. But I see that your feelings are hurt, so please do not talk about any larger or more monstrous issues than these suspicions.

OTHELLO: I will not.

IAGO: If you did, my lord, I would say terrible things that I would regret. Cassio is my worthy friend—My lord, I see you are sad.

OTHELLO: No, not really sad. I believe Desdemona is honest.

IAGO: May she have a long, honest life and may you continue trusting her for a long time!

OTHELLO: And yet, how nature makes mistakes—

IAGO: Yes, also there is the point that—if I may speak openly with you– she had turned down the many offers of marriage from people from her own country, color, and social position: you would think, that this is the natural course of things. Pew! One can smell a rotting, disgusting imbalance that goes against nature. But excuse me. I am not talking specifically about

Foul disproportion, thoughts unnatural.
But pardon me. I do not in position
Distinctly speak of her; though I may fear,
265   Her will, recoiling to her better judgement,
May fall to match you with her country forms,
And happily repent.

OTHELLO: Farewell, farewell:
If more thou dost perceive, let me know more;
270   Set on thy wife to observe. Leave me, Iago.

IAGO: *[Going.]* My lord, I take my leave.

OTHELLO: Why did I marry? This honest creature doubtless
Sees and knows more, much more, than he unfolds.

IAGO: *[Returning.]* My lord, I would I might entreat your honor
275   To scan this thing no further; leave it to time:
Though it be fit that Cassio have his place,
For sure he fills it up with great ability,
Yet, if you please to hold him off awhile,
You shall by that perceive him and his means:
280   Note if your lady strain his entertainment
With any strong or vehement importunity;
Much will be seen in that. In the meantime,
Let me be thought too busy in my fears—
As worthy cause I have to fear I am—
285   And hold her free, I do beseech your honor.

OTHELLO: Fear not my government.

IAGO: I once more take my leave.   *[Exit.]*

OTHELLO: This fellow's of exceeding honesty,
And knows all qualities, with a learned spirit,
290   Of human dealings. If I do prove her haggard,
Though that her jesses were my dear heartstrings,

Desdemona. I am afraid her disposition, rebelling against her better judgment, might try to compare you against her own people and regret her decision to have married.

OTHELLO: *Farewell, farewell. If you think of anything else, let me know. Get your wife to watch Desdemona. Let me be, Iago.*

IAGO: *[Going] My lord, I take my leave.*

OTHELLO: *Why did I get married? This honest creature no doubt sees and knows more, much more, than he reveals.*

IAGO: *[Returning] My lord, I wonder if I could get you to stop thinking about this and just give it time to work out. Even though it is appropriate that Cassio have his position—because he definitely has the ability, perhaps if you wait to reinstate him, you will learn more about him and his intentions. Take note if your lady, with strong persistence, insists that you entertain and listen to him. A great deal will be revealed by that. In the meantime, you should think that I am too preoccupied by my own fears—which I believe I am—and regard her as innocent; I do beg your honor.*

OTHELLO: *Do not fear my self control.*

IAGO: *I will leave you once more.*   [Exit]

OTHELLO: *This fellow is extremely honest, and is educated in all the qualities of human behavior. If I do prove that she is a wild hawk, even though her leashes are the strings attached to my heart, I will let her go and allow her to survive on her own and live as she wishes. Perhaps, because I am black*

133

I'ld whistle her off and let her down the wind
To prey at fortune. Haply, for I am black
And have not those soft parts of conversation
295   That chamberers have, or for I am declined
Into the vale of years—yet that's not much—
She's gone. I am abused, and my relief
Must be to loathe her. O curse of marriage,
That we can call these delicate creatures ours,
300   And not their appetites! I had rather be a toad,
And live upon the vapor of a dungeon,
Than keep a corner in the thing I love
For others' uses. Yet, 'tis the plague of great ones;
Prerogatived are they less than the base;
305   'Tis destiny unshunnable, like death:
Even then this forked plague is fated to us
When we do quicken. Desdemona comes:

[Reenter Desdemona and Emilia.]
If she be false, O, then heaven mocks itself!
I'll not believe't.

310   DESD: How now, my dear Othello!
Your dinner, and the generous islanders
By you invited, do attend your presence.

OTHELLO: I am to blame.

DESD: Why do you speak so faintly?
315   Are you not well?

OTHELLO: I have a pain upon my forehead here.

DESD: Faith, that's with watching; 'twill away again:
Let me but bind it hard, within this hour
It will be well.

134

and do not have the eloquence to speak like a gentleman and because I am older—there aren't many other reasons—she's gone. I have been wronged, and my relief will be to despise her. Oh, the curse of marriage is that we can call these delicate creatures ours, but not their desires! I would rather be a toad and live on the foul gases of a dungeon, than to have only a part of what I love and allow the rest to be used by others. But, that is the plague of great ones. They have fewer choices than the common people. It is an unavoidable destiny, like death. Being a victim of adultery is given to many men when we are born. Here comes Desdemona.

[Reenter Desdemona and Emilia]
If she is unfaithful, then heaven mocks itself! I will not believe it.

DESD: *Greetings, my dear Othello! Your dinner and the generous islanders who you invited are waiting for you.*

OTHELLO: *It is my fault.*

DESD: *Why do you speak so quietly? Are you sick?*

OTHELLO: *I have a headache.*

DESD: *By my faith, it's from too much work; it will go away soon. Let me bandage it well, and within an hour, it will subside.*

135

320 OTHELLO: Your napkin is too little;

[He puts the handkerchief from him, and she drops it.]

Let it alone. Come, I'll go in with you.

DESD: I am very sorry that you are not well.

[Exeunt Othello and Desdemona]

EMILIA: I am glad I have found this napkin:

This was her first remembrance from the Moor:

325   My wayward husband hath a hundred times

Woo'd me to steal it; but she so loves the token,

For he conjured her she should ever keep it,

That she reserves it evermore about her

To kiss and talk to. I'll have the work ta'en out,

330   And give't Iago. What he will do with it

Heaven knows, not I;

I nothing but to please his fantasy.

[Reenter Iago]

IAGO: How now, what do you here alone?

EMILIA: Do not you chide; I have a thing for you.

335 IAGO: A thing for me? It is a common thing—

EMILIA: Ha!

IAGO: To have a foolish wife.

EMILIA: O, is that all? What will you give me now

For that same handkerchief?

340 IAGO: What handkerchief?

EMILIA: What handkerchief?

Why, that the Moor first gave to Desdemona;

That which so often you did bid me steal.

136

OTHELLO: *Your napkin is too small:* [He pushes the handkerchief away from his head, and Desdemona drops it on the floor] *Leave it alone. Come, I'll go in with you.*

DESD: *I am very sorry that you are not well.*

[Exit Othello and Desdemona]

EMILIA: *I am glad I have found this handkerchief. This was Desdemona's first gift from Othello. My unreasonable husband has tried to get me to steal it a hundred times, but she loves the token so much. He told her that she should always keep it, so she always has it with her to kiss and talk to. I'll have the embroidery copied and give the duplicate to Iago; only heaven knows what he intends to do with it. I want only to please his whim.*

[Reenter Iago]

IAGO: *Greetings! What are you doing here alone?*

EMILIA: *Don't scold me. I have something for you.*

IAGO: *Something for me? It is something ordinary—*

EMILIA: *Ha!*

IAGO: *What a foolish wife.*

EMILIA: *Oh, is that all? What will you give me for the same handkerchief?*

IAGO: *What handkerchief?*

EMILIA: *What handkerchief? Why, the first gift from the Moor to Desdemona, the one you have asked me to steal so often.*

IAGO: Hast stol'n it from her?

345 EMILIA: No, faith; she let it drop by negligence,
  And, to the advantage, I being here took't up.
  Look, here it is.

IAGO: A good wench; give it me.

EMILIA: What will you do with't, that you have been so earnest
350 To have me filch it?

IAGO: *[Snatching it.]* Why, what is that to you?

EMILIA: If't be not for some purpose of import,
  Give't me again. Poor lady, she'll run mad
  When she shall lack it.

355 IAGO: Be not acknown on't; I have use for it.
  Go, leave me.   *[Exit Emilia.]*
  I will in Cassio's lodging lose this napkin,
  And let him find it. Trifles light as air
  Are to the jealous confirmations strong
360 As proofs of holy writ; this may do something.
  The Moor already changes with my poison:
  Dangerous conceits are in their natures poisons,
  Which at the first are scarce found to distaste,
  But with a little act upon the blood
365 Burn like the mines of sulphur. I did say so:
  Look, where he comes!

[Reenter Othello]
  Not poppy, nor mandragora,
  Nor all the drowsy syrups of the world,
  Shall ever medicine thee to that sweet sleep
370 Which thou owedst yesterday.

OTHELLO: Ha, ha, false to me?

IAGO: *Have you stolen it from her?*

EMILIA: *No. She dropped it by accident, and, luckily, I, being here, picked it up. Look, here it is.*

IAGO: *What a good girl. Give it to me.*

EMILIA: *What will you do with it; why were you so eager to have me steal it?*

IAGO: [Snatching it] *Why does that matter to you?*

EMILIA: *If it is not for some important purpose, give it back to me. The poor lady will go mad when she realizes it is missing.*

IAGO: *Don't say anything about this. I have a use for it. Go, leave me.*
                                                        [Exit Emilia]
I will place this handkerchief in Cassio's apartment and let him find it. Small items, as light as air, will confirm what jealous people believe and give them proof that is as unquestionable as the words of Holy Scripture. The Moor has already changed since I poisoned his thoughts with suspicions. Ideas are as dangerous as poison in their own way because at first they seem only a little sour, but when they begin to work in the blood, they burn like sulfur mines. Look, here he comes!

[Reenter Othello]
No sleep-inducing plants like poppies or mandrake, nor all the sleeping potions in the world, will ever give you, Othello, the sweet, deep sleep that you had yesterday.

OTHELLO: *Ha! ha! Lying to me?*

139

IAGO: Why, how now, general! No more of that.

OTHELLO: Avaunt! be gone! Thou hast set me on the rack:
I swear 'tis better to be much abused
375   Than but to know't a little.

IAGO: How now, my lord?

OTHELLO: What sense had I of her stol'n hours of lust?
I saw't not, thought it not, it harm'd not me;
I slept the next night well, was free and merry;
380   I found not Cassio's kisses on her lips:
He that is robb'd, not wanting what is stol'n,
Let him not know't and he's not robb'd at all.

IAGO: I am sorry to hear this.

OTHELLO: I had been happy if the general camp,
385   Pioners and all, had tasted her sweet body,
So I had nothing known. O, now forever
Farewell the tranquil mind! Farewell content!
Farewell the plumed troop and the big wars
That make ambition virtue! O, farewell,
390   Farewell the neighing steed and the shrill trump,
The spiritstirring drum, the earpiercing fife,
The royal banner, and all quality,
Pride, pomp, and circumstance of glorious war!
And O you mortal engines, whose rude throats
395   The immortal Jove's dread clamors counterfeit,
Farewell! Othello's occupation's gone!

IAGO: Is't possible, my lord?

OTHELLO: Villain, be sure thou prove my love a whore;
Be sure of it. Give me the ocular proof;
400   Or, by the worth of man's eternal soul,
Thou hadst been better have been born a dog
Than answer my waked wrath!

IAGO: Why, hello, general! No more of that kind of talk.

OTHELLO: Go! Be gone! You have put me on the torturing rack. I swear it is better to be deceived than it is to know even a little.

IAGO: What do you mean, my lord?

OTHELLO: What did I know about her secret hours of lust? I didn't see it, didn't think about it, and it did not hurt me. I slept well last night, was free and happy. I did not find Cassio's kisses on her lips. A person may be robbed, but if he has no knowledge of what has been stolen, ultimately, he has not been robbed at all.

IAGO: I am sorry to hear this.

OTHELLO: I would have been happier if every soldier in camp had tasted her sweet body, and I had known nothing about it. Oh, now, good-bye forever to the peaceful mind! Good-bye contentment! Farewell to the decorated troops and the big wars that make ambition an asset! Oh, farewell! Farewell the neighing horse, the screeching trumpet, the spirit-stirring drum, the ear-piercing flute, the royal banner, and all quality, pride, magnificence, and customs of glorious war! And, oh, you cannons, whose rude throats mimic the immortal Jove's thunder, farewell! Othello's occupation is gone!

IAGO: Is it possible, my lord?

OTHELLO: Villain, be sure you can prove that my love is a whore. [Grabbing Othello by the throat.] Be sure of it. Give me proof I can see, or by the worth of man's eternal soul, you will wish that you were born a dog rather than to be forced to answer to my awakened rage!

141

IAGO: Is't come to this?

OTHELLO: Make me to see't; or at the least so prove it,
405   That the probation bear no hinge nor loop
To hang a doubt on; or woe upon thy life!

IAGO: My noble lord

OTHELLO: If thou dost slander her and torture me,
Never pray more; abandon all remorse;
410   On horror's head horrors accumulate.
Do deeds to make heaven weep, all earth amazed;
For nothing canst thou to damnation add
Greater than that.

IAGO: O grace! O heaven defend me!
415   Are you a man? have you a soul or sense?
God be wi' you; take mine office. O wretched fool,
That livest to make thine honesty a vice!
O monstrous world! Take note, take note, O world,
To be direct and honest is not safe.
420   I thank you for this profit, and from hence
I'll love no friend sith love breeds such offense.

OTHELLO: Nay, stay; thou shouldst be honest.

IAGO: I should be wise; for honesty's a fool,
And loses that it works for.

425 OTHELLO: By the world,
I think my wife be honest, and think she is not;
I think that thou art just, and think thou art not.
I'll have some proof. Her name, that was as fresh
As Dian's visage, is now begrimed and black
430   As mine own face. If there be cords or knives,
Poison or fire, or suffocating streams,
I'll not endure it. Would I were satisfied!

IAGO: Has it come to this?

OTHELLO: Make me see it, or at least prove it. Prove that your investigation leaves no tiny room for doubt, or your life will be miserable!

IAGO: My noble lord—

OTHELLO: If you lie about her and torture me, prayer will not help you, so abandon your conscience. On horror's head more horrors will gather. You may do deeds that make the heavens weep and confuse the world. There is nothing you can do, however, to add to your damnation that will be greater than this.

IAGO: Oh, grace! Oh, heaven defend me! Are you a man? Have you a soul or sense? God be with you; take away my position. Oh, what a miserable fool I am that I should live to make my honesty a weakness! Oh, monstrous world! Take note, take note, oh, world; to be direct and honest is not safe. I thank you for this lesson, and from now on I will not love a friend, since love leads to such an accusation.

OTHELLO: No, stay. You need to be honest.

IAGO: I should be wise; being honest is foolish because it ends up losing what it is working for.

OTHELLO: For the entire world, I think my wife is honest and yet think she is not. I think that you are just and yet think you are not. I need some proof. Her name, which was as fresh as a vision of Diana, is now dirty and black as my own face. If cords or knives, poison or fire, or suffocating streams were available, I wouldn't endure this. I must be satisfied!

IAGO: I see, sir, you are eaten up with passion;
    I do repent me that I put it to you.
435   You would be satisfied?

OTHELLO: Would? Nay, I will.

IAGO: And may. But, how? how satisfied, my lord?
    Would you, the supervisor, grossly gape on?
    Behold her topp'd?

440   OTHELLO: Death and damnation! O!

IAGO: It were a tedious difficulty, I think,
    To bring them to that prospect. Damn them then,
    If ever mortal eyes do see them bolster
    More than their own! What then? how then?
445   What shall I say? Where's satisfaction?
    It is impossible you should see this
    Were they as prime as goats, as hot as monkeys,
    As salt as wolves in pride, and fools as gross
    As ignorance made drunk. But yet, I say,
    If imputation and strong circumstances,
450   Which lead directly to the door of truth,
    Will give you satisfaction, you may have't.

OTHELLO: Give me a living reason she's disloyal.

IAGO: I do not like the office;
    But sith I am enter'd in this cause so far,
    Prick'd to't by foolish honesty and love,
455   I will go on. I lay with Cassio lately
    And, being troubled with a raging tooth,
    I could not sleep.
    There are a kind of men so loose of soul,
    That in their sleeps will mutter their affairs;
460   One of this kind is Cassio
    In sleep I heard him say, "Sweet Desdemona,

IAGO: I see, sir, that you are consumed with passion.
    I am sorry that I ever spoke of this. How would you be satisfied?

OTHELLO: Would be? No, I will be.

IAGO: Yes, but, how? What would satisfy you my lord? Would you like some
    kind of spectator to stare disgustedly at them in the act?

OTHELLO: Death and damnation! Oh!

IAGO: It would be extremely difficult, I think, to bring that into view. Damn
    them; only if mortal eyes, other than their own, see them committing adul-
    tery. What then? How then? What should I say? How will you be satisfied?
    It is impossible for you to see this, even if they were as eager as goats, as hot
    as monkeys, as lustful as wolves in pride, and as foolish as drunken idiots.
    But, I say, if rumors and strong circumstantial evidence that leads directly
    to the truth, will give you satisfaction, you may have it.

OTHELLO: Give me a real example of her disloyalty.

IAGO: I do not like this job. But, since I am involved this much, pushed forward
    by foolish honesty and love, I will go on. I have slept next to Cassio lately,
    and, being bothered with a toothache, I could not sleep. Some men, whose
    souls are so relaxed, mumble the secrets they keep while they sleep. Cassio
    is like that. In his sleep I heard him say, "Sweet Desdemona, let's be careful,
    we have to hide our love." Then, sir, he gripped and squeezed my hand and
    cried, "Oh, sweet creature!" and then he kissed me hard, as if kisses grew on
    my lips and he were picking them by the roots. Then he laid his leg over my
    thigh, and sighed, and kissed; then he cried, "What a tragic fate that you are
    married to the Moor!"

Let us be wary, let us hide our loves";
And then, sir, would he gripe and wring my hand,
Cry, "O sweet creature!" and then kiss me hard,
465 As if he pluck'd up kisses by the roots,
That grew upon my lips; then laid his leg
Over my thigh, and sigh'd and kiss'd; and then
Cried, "Cursed fate that gave thee to the Moor!"

OTHELLO: O monstrous! monstrous!

470 IAGO: Nay, this was but his dream.

OTHELLO: But this denoted a foregone conclusion:
'Tis a shrewd doubt, though it be but a dream.

IAGO: And this may help to thicken other proofs
That do demonstrate thinly.

475 OTHELLO: I'll tear her all to pieces.

IAGO: Nay, but be wise; yet we see nothing done;
She may be honest yet. Tell me but this;
Have you not sometimes seen a handkerchief
Spotted with strawberries in your wife's hand?

480 OTHELLO: I gave her such a one; 'twas my first gift.

IAGO: I know not that; but such a handkerchief—
I am sure it was your wife's—did I today
See Cassio wipe his beard with.

OTHELLO: If it be that—

485 IAGO: If it be that, or any that was hers,
It speaks against her with the other proofs.

OTHELLO: O, that the slave had forty thousand lives!

OTHELLO: *Oh, monstrous, monstrous!*

IAGO: *No, remember this was only his dream.*

OTHELLO: *But, it represents previous occurrence. Even though it is only a dream, it raises questions.*

IAGO: *And this may help to reinforce other evidence, which is not enough by itself.*

OTHELLO: *I'll tear her to pieces.*

IAGO: *No, be wise. We still have not seen anything done. She may still be honorable. Tell me this: Have you ever seen your wife holding a handkerchief embroidered with strawberries?*

OTHELLO: *I gave her a handkerchief like that. It was my first gift.*

IAGO: *I didn't know that, but a handkerchief like that—I am sure it was your wife's—I saw Cassio wipe his beard with today.*

OTHELLO: *If it was that one—*

IAGO: *If it was that handkerchief or any of hers, it is proof, along with everything else.*

OTHELLO: *Oh, I wish that the slave had forty thousand lives! One lifetime is not*

One is too poor, too weak for my revenge.
Now do I see 'tis true. Look here, Iago;
490   All my fond love thus do I blow to heaven:
'Tis gone.
Arise, black vengeance, from thy hollow cell!
Yield up, O love, thy crown and hearted throne
To tyrannous hate! Swell, bosom, with thy fraught,
495   For 'tis of aspics' tongues!

IAGO: Yet be content.

OTHELLO: O, blood, blood, blood!

IAGO: Patience, I say; your mind perhaps may change.

OTHELLO: Never, Iago: Like to the Pontic Sea,
500   Whose icy current and compulsive course
Ne'er feels retiring ebb, but keeps due on
To the Propontic and the Hellespont,
Even so my bloody thoughts, with violent pace,
Shall ne'er look back, ne'er ebb to humble love,
505   Till that a capable and wide revenge
Swallow them up. Now, by yond marble heaven,
In the due reverence of a sacred vow
[Kneels.] I here engage my words.

IAGO: Do not rise yet.
510   *[Kneels.]* Witness, you everburning lights above,
You elements that clip us round about,
Witness that here Iago doth give up
The execution of his wit, hands, heart,
To wrong'd Othello's service! Let him command,
515   And to obey shall be in me remorse,
What bloody business ever.   *[They rise.]*

OTHELLO: I greet thy love,
Not with vain thanks, but with acceptance bounteous, And will
upon the instant put thee to't:

enough for me to get revenge. Now I see it is true. Look here, Iago, all my love for Cassio I now throw up to heaven. It is gone. My dark revenge, rise up from your hollow cell! Oh, love, give up your crown and precious throne for cruel hatred! May my heart swell with this burden made from the tongues of poisonous snakes.

IAGO: Now calm down.

OTHELLO: Oh, blood, blood, blood!

IAGO: Have patience, I say; perhaps you will change your mind.

OTHELLO: Never, Iago. I am like the Black Sea, whose icy and forward current never has a retreating tide but keeps heading toward its destination and toward the Hellespont. My bloody thoughts, also rushing at a violent pace, will never look back, will never retreat to kind love until a suitable and all-encompassing revenge swallows Cassio and Desdemona up. Now, by far-off heaven, paying the highest respect to a sacred promise, [Kneels] I pledge my word.

IAGO: Do not get up yet. [Kneels] *You perpetual lights above, the wind and air that circle around us, witness and testify to the fact that Iago gives up the use of his will, his hands, his heart, to the betrayed Othello! Let Othello command, and I will obey and do whatever bloody business he asks.*

OTHELLO: I welcome your love, not with worthless thanks, but with openhearted approval, and I will give you a job this very instant. Within three days let me hear you say that Cassio is dead.

520   Within these three days let me hear thee say
           That Cassio's not alive.

IAGO: My friend is dead, 'tis done at your request;
           But let her live.

OTHELLO: Damn her, lewd minx! O, damn her!
525   Come, go with me apart; I will withdraw,
           To furnish me with some swift means of death
           For the fair devil. Now art thou my lieutenant.

IAGO: I am your own forever.

[Exeunt.]

SCENE 4
Before the castle.

[Enter Desdemona, Emilia, and Clown.]

DESD: Do you know, sirrah, where Lieutenant Cassio lies?

CLOWN. I dare not say he lies anywhere.

DESD: Why, man?

CLOWN. He's a soldier; and for one to say a soldier lies, is stabbing.

5   DESD: Go to! Where lodges he?

CLOWN. To tell you where he lodges, is to tell you where I lie.

DESD: Can anything be made of this?

CLOWN. I know not where he lodges, and for me to devise a lodging, and say he lies here or he lies there, were to lie in mine own throat.

IAGO: My friend is dead. It is done at your request; but let Desdemona live.

OTHELLO: Damn her, lustful, wild woman! Oh, damn her! Come with me; I will leave, to think of some swift means of death for the beautiful devil. Now you are my lieutenant.

IAGO: I am your loyal servant forever.
                              [Exeunt]

SCENE IV
In front of the castle.

[Enter Desdemona, Emilia, and Clown]

DESD: Do you know, sir, where Lieutenant Cassio lies?

CLOWN: I cannot say that he lies anywhere.

DESD: What, man?

CLOWN: He is a soldier, and to say a soldier lies is stabbing him.

DESD: All right. Where is he staying?

CLOWN: To tell you where he is staying, is to tell you where I lie.

DESD: Can anything be made of this nonsense?

CLOWN: I do not know where he stays, and for me to invent a place and say he lies here or he lies there would be my own lie.

10   DESD: Can you inquire him out and be edified by report?

CLOWN. I will catechize the world for him; that is, make questions and
   by them answer.

DESD: Seek him, bid him come hither. Tell him I have moved my lord
   on his behalf and hope all will be well.

15   CLOWN. To do this is within the compass of man's wit, and therefore I
   will attempt the doing it.   *[Exit.]*

DESD: Where should I lose that handkerchief, Emilia?

EMILIA: I know not, madam.

DESD: Believe me, I had rather have lost my purse
20   Full of crusadoes; and, but my noble Moor
      Is true of mind and made of no such baseness
      As jealous creatures are, it were enough
      To put him to ill thinking.

EMILIA: Is he not jealous?

25   DESD: Who, he? I think the sun where he was born
      Drew all such humors from him.

EMILIA: Look, where he comes.

DESD: I will not leave him now till Cassio
      Be call'd to him.

[Enter Othello.]
30   How is't with you, my lord?

OTHELLO: Well, my good lady. *[Aside.]* O, hardness to dissemble!
      How do you, Desdemona?

152

DESD: *Can you find out where he is and inform me?*

CLOWN: *I will quiz the world for him. That is, I will make up questions and find answers.*

DESD: *Look for him, and ask him to come here. Tell him I have convinced my lord on his behalf, and I hope all will be well.*

CLOWN: *To do this is within the range of man's abilities, and, therefore, I will attempt to do it.* [Exit]

DESD: *Where did I lose that handkerchief, Emilia?*

EMILIA: *I don't know, madam.*

DESD: *Believe me, I would rather have lost my purse full of gold coins. But my noble Moor has a clear mind and does not have the kind of meanness that jealous people have. If he were, this would be enough to make him think the worst.*

EMILIA: *He is not jealous?*

DESD: *Who, Othello? I think the sunny climate where he was born drew all such ill-temper out of him.*

EMILIA: *Look, here he comes.*

DESD: *I will stay with Othello now until he calls Cassio here.*

[Enter Othello]
How are you, my lord?

OTHELLO: *I am well, my good lady.*
[Aside] *Oh, it is difficult to lie! How are you, Desdemona?*

DESD: Well, my good lord.

OTHELLO: Give me your hand. This hand is moist, my lady.

35 DESD: It yet has felt no age nor known no sorrow:

OTHELLO: This argues fruitfulness and liberal heart;
    Hot, hot, and moist. This hand of yours requires
    A sequester from liberty, fasting and prayer,
    Much castigation, exercise devout,
40   For here's a young and sweating devil here
    That commonly rebels. 'Tis a good hand,
    A frank one.

DESD: You may, indeed, say so;
    For 'twas that hand that gave away my heart.

45 OTHELLO: A liberal hand. The hearts of old gave hands;
    But our new heraldry is hands, not hearts.

DESD: I cannot speak of this. Come now, your promise.

OTHELLO: What promise, chuck?

DESD: I have sent to bid Cassio come speak with you.

50 OTHELLO: I have a salt and sorry rheum offends me;
    Lend me thy handkerchief.

DESD: Here, my lord.

OTHELLO: That which I gave you.

DESD: I have it not about me.

55 OTHELLO: Not?

DESD: Well, my good lord.

OTHELLO: Give me your hand. This hand is damp, my lady.

DESD: It has not felt age or sorrow yet.

OTHELLO: This damp hand indicates generosity and a kind heart. Hot, hot, and moist. This hand of yours requires a separation from liberty, fasting and prayer, a lot of purification, and devout prayers. Yes, this hand is a young and sweating devil that usually rebels. It is a good hand, a honest hand.

DESD: You may accurately say so, because it was that hand that gave my heart away.

OTHELLO: A generous hand. At one time, people used to marry out of love, but now, marriage has become a formality, a kind of shallow ceremony, where hands are given away, not hearts.

DESD: I cannot speak about this. Come now; remember your promise.

OTHELLO: What promise, my dear?

DESD: I have sent for Cassio to come and speak with you.

OTHELLO: I am teary, and an awful cold bothers me. Lend me your handkerchief.

DESD: Here, my lord.

OTHELLO: The one which I gave you.

DESD: I do not have it with me

OTHELLO: No?

DESD: No, faith, my lord.

OTHELLO: That's a fault. That handkerchief
    Did an Egyptian to my mother give;
    She was a charmer, and could almost read
60   The thoughts of people. She told her, while she kept it,
    'Twould make her amiable and subdue my father
    Entirely to her love, but if she lost it
    Or made a gift of it, my father's eye
    Should hold her loathed and his spirits should hunt
65   After new fancies. She dying gave it me,
    And bid me, when my fate would have me wive,
    To give it her. I did so, and take heed on't;
    Make it a darling like your precious eye;
    To lose't or give't away were such perdition
70   As nothing else could match.

DESD: Is't possible?

OTHELLO: 'Tis true; there's magic in the web of it.
    A sibyl, that had number'd in the world
    The sun to course two hundred compasses,
75   In her prophetic fury sew'd the work;
    The worms were hallow'd that did breed the silk,
    And it was dyed in mummy which the skillful
    Conserved of maidens' hearts.

DESD: Indeed! is't true?

80 OTHELLO: Most veritable; therefore look to't well.

DESD: Then would to God that I had never seen't!

OTHELLO: Ha! wherefore?

DESD: Why do you speak so startingly and rash?

DESD: No, indeed, my lord.

OTHELLO: That is a mistake. An Egyptian gave that handkerchief to my mother. She was a psychic and could almost read people's thoughts. She told my mother that the handkerchief would make her sweet, and my father would be completely controlled by her love. But if she lost it or gave it away, my father would see only hatred for her, and he would hunt after new lovers. My mother gave it to me on her deathbed and told me that when it was time for me to marry, I should give it to my wife. I did so; and seriously consider this, make it as cherished as your precious eyesight. To lose it or give it away would cause such disaster that nothing else could match it.

DESD: Is this possible?

OTHELLO: It is true. There is magic in the knitting of it. A fortune-teller who lived for two hundred years sewed the handkerchief in a prophetic fury. Holy worms spun the silk, and it was dyed in a fluid made from skillfully preserved maidens' hearts.

DESD: Honestly! Is this true?

OTHELLO: Absolutely true. Therefore, take good care of it.

DESD: Then I wish to God that I had never seen it!

OTHELLO: Ha! Why?

DESD: Why are you speaking so frighteningly and recklessly?

OTHELLO: Is't lost? is't gone? speak, is it out o' the way?

85   DESD: Heaven bless us!

OTHELLO: Say you?

DESD: It is not lost; but what an if it were?

OTHELLO: How?

DESD: I say, it is not lost.

90   OTHELLO: Fetch't, let me see it.

DESD: Why, so I can, sir, but I will not now.
    This is a trick to put me from my suit.
    Pray you, let Cassio be received again.

OTHELLO: Fetch me the handkerchief, my mind misgives.

95   DESD: Come, come; You'll never meet a more sufficient man.

OTHELLO: The handkerchief!

DESD: I pray, talk me of Cassio:

OTHELLO: The handkerchief!

DESD: A man that all his time
100   Hath founded his good fortunes on your love,
    Shared dangers with you—

OTHELLO: The handkerchief!

DESD: In sooth, you are to blame.

OTHELLO: Away!   *[Exit.]*

OTHELLO: *Is it lost? Is it gone? Speak up; is it put away?*

DESD: *Heaven bless us!*

OTHELLO: *What do you say?*

DESD: *It is not lost, but what if it were?*

OTHELLO: *How?*

DESD: *I say, it is not lost.*

OTHELLO: *Get it, let me see it.*

DESD: *Well, I can get it, sir, but not now. This is a trick to distract me from my cause. I beg you, let Cassio speak to you.*

OTHELLO: *Get me the handkerchief. My mind tells me that evil is present.*

DESD: *Come, come. You will never meet a better man than Cassio.*

OTHELLO: *The handkerchief!*

DESD: *I beg you, talk to me about Cassio.*

OTHELLO: *The handkerchief!*

DESD: *A man that, at all times, has based his good fortunes on your love, shared dangers with you—*

OTHELLO: *The handkerchief!*

DESD: *In truth, you are to blame.*

OTHELLO: *I'm leaving!*   [Exit]

159

105   EMILIA: Is not this man jealous?

DESD: I ne'er saw this before.
   Sure there's some wonder in this handkerchief;
   I am most unhappy in the loss of it.

EMILIA: 'Tis not a year or two shows us a man:
110   They are all but stomachs and we all but food;
   They eat us hungerly, and when they are full
   They belch us. Look you! Cassio and my husband.

[Enter Cassio and Iago.]

IAGO: There is no other way; 'tis she must do't:
   And, lo, the happiness! Go and importune her.

115   DESD: How now, good Cassio! What's the news with you?

CASSIO: Madam, my former suit: I do beseech you
   That by your virtuous means I may again
   Exist and be a member of his love
   Whom I with all the office of my heart
120   Entirely honor. I would not be delay'd.
   If my offense be of such mortal kind
   That nor my service past nor present sorrows
   Nor purposed merit in futurity
   Can ransom me into his love again,
125   But to know so must be my benefit;
   So shall I clothe me in a forced content
   And shut myself up in some other course
   To Fortune's alms.

DESD: Alas, thrice gentle Cassio!
130   My advocation is not now in tune;
   My lord is not my lord, nor should I know him
   Were he in favor as in humor alter'd.
   So help me every spirit sanctified,

BOTH: Yes, sir, we hope.

DOGBERRY: Write down that they hope that they serve God; but write God first, for God defend but that God should go before such villains! Sirs, it has been already proved that you are little better than false knaves, and it will be thought so directly. How do you answer the charge?

CONRADE: Well, sir, we say we are not.

DOGBERRY: A very witty man, I assure you; but I will deal with him. Come here, sir. One word in your ear. Sir, I say to you, it is thought that you are lying knaves.

BORACHIO: Sir, I say to you we are not.

DOGBERRY: Well, stand back. Before God, they both tell the same story. Have you written down that they are not false knaves?

SEXTON: Master constable, you are not examining correctly; you must question the watch for they are the accusers.

DOGBERRY: Yes, indeed, that's the easiest way. Let the watch step forward. Sirs, I order you in the name of the prince to accuse these men.

FIRST WATCHMAN: This man said that Don John, the prince's brother, was a criminal.

DOGBERRY: Write down that Prince Don John is a criminal. Why this is flat perjury to call a prince's brother villain.

BORACHIO: Master constable—

DOGBERRY: Pray thee, fellow, peace. I do not like thy look, I promise thee.

40 SEXTON: What heard you him say else?

SECOND WATCHMAN: Marry, that he had received a thousand ducats
of Don John for accusing the Lady Hero wrongfully.

DOGBERRY: Flat burglary as ever was committed.

VERGES: Yea, by the mass, that it is.

45 SEXTON: What else, fellow?

FIRST WATCHMAN: And that Count Claudio did mean, upon his
words, to disgrace Hero before the whole assembly, and not
marry her.

DOGBERRY: O villain! thou wilt be condemned into everlasting
50   redemption for this.

SEXTON: What else?

WATCHMEN: This is all.

SEXTON: And this is more, masters, than you can deny. Prince Don
55   John is this morning secretly stolen away. Hero was in this
manner accused, in this manner refused, and upon the grief of
this suddenly died. Master constable, let these men be bound
and brought to Leonato's. I will go before and show him their
examination. [Exit.]

DOGBERRY: Excuse me, fellow, quiet. I do not like your looks, I assure you.

SEXTON: What else did you hear him say?

SECOND WATCHMAN: Well, that he had received a thousand gold coins from Don John for wrongly accusing Lady Hero.

DOGBERRY: Flat burglary[4] as any ever committed.

VERGES: Yes, indeed, that it is.

SEXTON: What else, fellow?

FIRST WATCHMAN: And that Count Claudio meant, by his own words, to disgrace Hero in front of the whole congregation and not marry her.

DOGBERRY: Oh villain! You'll be condemned to everlasting redemption[5] for this.

SEXTON: What else?

WATCHMEN: That's all.

SEXTON: And this is more, masters, than you can deny. Prince Don John this morning has secretly left town. Hero was accused, and in this way refused, and has died from her grief. Master constable, bind these men and bring them to Leonato's house. I'll go ahead and show him this examination. [Sexton leaves.]

4. burglary - perhaps he meant perjury
5. redemption - perdition

DOGBERRY: Come, let them be opinioned.

60 VERGES: Let them be in the hands—

CONRADE: Off, coxcomb!

DOGBERRY: God's my life, where's the sexton? Let him write down
the prince's officer coxcomb. Come, bind them—Thou naughty varlet!

65 CONRADE: Away! you are an ass, you are an ass.

DOGBERRY: Dost thou not suspect my place? Dost thou not suspect
my years? O that he were here to write me down an ass! But,
masters, remember that I am an ass. Though it be not written
down, yet forget not that I am an ass. No, thou villain, thou
70   art full of piety, as shall be proved upon thee by good witness. I am a wise fellow; and which is more, an officer; and
which is more, a householder; and which is more, as pretty
a piece of flesh as any is in Messina, and one that knows the
law, go to! and a rich fellow enough, go to! and a fellow that
75   hath had losses; and one that hath two gowns and everything
handsome about him. Bring him away. O that I had been writ
down an ass!

[Exeunt.]

DOGBERRY: Here, let them be opinioned[6].

VERGES: Let them be in the hands—

CONRADE: Stop, fool!

DOGBERRY: Good God, where's the sexton. Let him write down that he called the prince's officer fool. Come, bind them—you naughty varlet.

CONRADE: Go away! You are an ass; you are an ass.

DOGBERRY: Don't you suspect[7] my position? Don't you suspect my age? Oh, if only the sexton were here to write me down an ass. But, sirs, remember that I am an ass. Even though it isn't written down, don't forget that I am an ass. No, you villain, you are full of piety[8] which will be proved by good witness. I am a wise fellow; and further, an officer and furthermore a home owner and furthermore as pretty piece of flesh a man as any in town; and one who knows the law, besides! And rich enough fellow, besides! And a man who has endured losses; and one who has two suits and everything fine about him. Bring him away. Oh, I wish I had been written down as an ass!

[Exit with the others.]

6. opinioned - pinioned, tied up
7. suspect - respect
8. piety - impiety

Act V

Scene 1
Before Leonato's House

[Enter Leonato and his brother Antonio.]

ANTONIO: If you go on thus, you will kill yourself,
        And 'tis not wisdom thus to second grief
        Against yourself.

LEONATO: I pray thee cease thy counsel,
5   Which falls into mine ears as profitless
        As water in a sieve. Give not me counsel,
        Nor let no comforter delight mine ear
        But such a one whose wrongs do suit with mine.
        Bring me a father that so loved his child,
10   Whose joy of her is overwhelmed like mine,
        And bid him speak to me of patience.
        Measure his woe the length and breadth of mine,
        And let it answer every strain for strain,
        As thus for thus, and such a grief for such,
15   In every lineament, branch, shape, and form.
        If such a one will smile and stroke his beard,
        Bid sorrow wag, cry 'hem' when he should groan,
        Patch grief with proverbs, make misfortune drunk
        With candle-wasters—bring him yet to me,
20   And I of him will gather patience.
        But there is no such man; for, brother, men
        Can counsel and speak comfort to that grief

Act V

Scene 1
Before Leonato's House

[Enter Leonato and his brother Antonio.]

ANTONIO: *If you go on this way, you will kill yourself. It isn't wise to support such grief against your own self.*

LEONATO: *Please stop this advice. Words in my ears are as wasted as water in a sieve. Don't give me advice or cheer me with any news, but that which is similar to mine. Bring me a father who loved his own child, whose love is overwhelming like mine, and have him talk of patience. Measure his grief with the size of mine, matching strain and heartache in every way. If someone like that will smile, bid sorrow depart, patch his grief with proverbs, philosophize on his misfortune, then bring him before me and I will be consoled. But there is no such man, for brother, men can comfort grief and counsel only to that that they cannot feel; but when tasting its reality their counsel turns passionate, where before was remedy, now is rage. Resist melancholy with beauty, relieve pain with talk, and sorrow with words. No, no! It's the duty of men to comfort those who writhe under sorrow's heavy load, but no man's virtue or aid is strong when he has sorrows that cry louder than advice.*

Which they themselves not feel; but, tasting it,
Their counsel turns to passion, which before
25 Would give preceptial medicine to rage,
Fetter strong madness in a silken thread,
Charm ache with air and agony with words.
No, no! 'Tis all men's office to speak patience
To those that wring under the load of sorrow,
30 But no man's virtue nor sufficiency
To be so moral when he shall endure
The like himself. Therefore give me no counsel.
My griefs cry louder than advertisement.

35 ANTONIO: Therein do men from children nothing differ.

LEONATO: I pray thee peace. I will be flesh and blood;
For there was never yet philosopher
That could endure the toothache patiently,
However they have writ the style of gods
40 And made a push at chance and sufferance.

ANTONIO: Yet bend not all the harm upon yourself. Make those that
do offend you suffer too.

LEONATO: There thou speak'st reason. Nay, I will do so.
45 My soul doth tell me Hero is belied;
And that shall Claudio know; so shall the prince,
And all of them that thus dishonour her.

[Enter Don Pedro and Claudio.]

ANTONIO: Here comes the prince and Claudio hastily.

DON PEDRO: Good den, good den.

55 CLAUDIO: Good day to both of you.

LEONATO: Hear you, my lords!

ANTONIO: *In this way, men do not differ from children.*

LEONATO: *Please, peace. I will be flesh and blood, for there was never yet a philosopher who could endure even a toothache patiently, no matter how they may have written like gods, nor scoffed at misfortune and suffering.*

ANTONIO: *Yet, don't put this whole burden on yourself. Make those who hurt you suffer also.*

LEONATO: *Now you speak reasonably. Yes, I will do that. My soul tells me that Hero is wronged, and that Claudio will know this; and so will the prince and all of those who thus dishonored her.*

[Enter Don Pedro and Claudio.]

ANTONIO: *Here comes the prince and Claudio in great haste.*

DON PEDRO: *Good evening, good evening.*

CLAUDIO: *Good day to both of you.*

LEONATO: *Hear me, my lords—*

DON PEDRO: We have some haste, Leonato.

LEONATO: Some haste, my lord! well, fare you well, my lord. Are
    you so hasty now? Well, all is one.

60 DON PEDRO: Nay, do not quarrel with us, good old man.

ANTONIO: If he could right himself with quarrelling,
    Some of us would lie low.

CLAUDIO: Who wrongs him?

LEONATO: Marry, thou dost wrong me, thou dissembler, thou!
65   Nay, never lay thy hand upon thy sword;
    I fear thee not.

CLAUDIO: Mary, beshrew my hand
    If it should give your age such cause of fear.
    In faith, my hand meant nothing to my sword.

70 LEONATO: Tush, tush, man! never fleer and jest at me.
    I speak not like a dotard nor a fool,
    As under privilege of age to brag
    What I have done being young, or what would do,
    Were I not old. Know, Claudio, to thy head,
75   Thou hast so wronged mine innocent child and me
    That I am forced to lay my reverence by
    And, with grey hairs and bruise of many days,
    Do challenge thee to trial of a man.
    I say thou hast belied mine innocent child;
80   Thy slander hath gone through and through her heart,
    And she lied buried with her ancestors;
    O, in a tomb where never scandal slept,
    Save this of hers, framed by thy villany!

CLAUDIO: My villany?

DON PEDRO: *We are in a hurry, Leonato.*

LEONATO: *Some haste, my lord. Well, good bye, my lord. Are you so hasty now? Well, it doesn't matter.*

DON PEDRO: *No, do not quarrel with us, good old man.*

ANTONIO: *If he could calm himself with quarrelling, some of us would be buried.*

CLAUDIO: *Who wrongs him?*

LEONATO: *Indeed, you wrong me, you deceiver! Don't put your hand upon your sword, I don't fear you.*

CLAUDIO: *Damn my hand if it should give your age some cause to fear. Truly, my hand meant nothing on my sword.*

LEONATO: *Shoot, man. Never snap and jest at me. I do not speak like an imbecile or fool, as the privilege of advanced age would allow me, bragging about youthful exploits or what I would do if I were not so old. Know this Claudio, deep in your mind; you have wronged an innocent child and me, so that I am forced to set aside my restraint, and with my gray hairs and wear from many years, do challenge you to a duel. I say that you have defiled my innocent child. Your slander has gone through to her heart, and she lies buried with her ancestors—in a tomb where scandal has never slept, except for her's, which was framed by your villainy!*

CLAUDIO: *My villainy?*

85   LEONATO: Thine, Claudio; thine I say.

DON PEDRO: You say not right, old man.

LEONATO: My lord, my lord, I'll prove it on his body if he dare,
        Despite his nice fence and his active practice,
        His May of youth and bloom of lustihood.

90   CLAUDIO: Away! I will not have to do with you.

LEONATO: Canst thou so daff me? Thou hast killed my child.
        If thou kill'st me, boy, thou shalt kill a man.

ANTONIO: He shall kill two of us, and men indeed.
        But that's no matter; let him kill one first.
95   Win me and wear me! Let him answer me.
        Come, follow me, boy.
        Come, sir boy, come follow me.
        Sir boy, I'll whip you from your foining fence!
        Nay, as I am a gentleman, I will.

100 LEONATO: Brother Anthony—

ANTONIO: Hold you content. What, man! I know them, yea,
        And what they weigh, even to the utmost scruple,
        Scambling, outfacing, fashion-monging boys,
        That lie and cog and flout, deprave and slander,
105   Go antiquely, and show outward hideousness,
        And speak off half a dozen dangerous words,
        How they might hurt their enemies, if they durst;
        And this is all.

LEONATO: But, brother Anthony—

110 ANTONIO: Come, 'tis no matter.
        Do not you meddle; let me deal in this.

LEONATO: *Yours, Claudio; yours I say.*

DON PEDRO: *You say not right, old man.*

LEONATO: *My lord, my lord, I'll prove it on his body if he dares, despite his clever sword play and his obvious practice, his youthfulness and bloom of strength.*

CLAUDIO: *Go away! I will not fight you.*

LEONATO: *You can't put me aside. You have killed my child. If you kill me, boy, then you will have killed a man.*

ANTONIO: *He shall kill two of us, and both men. But that's unimportant; let him kill me first. I challenge you! Let him answer me. Come, follow me, boy. Come, sir boy, come follow me. Sir boy, I'll whip you from your thrusting fence! Yes, as I am a gentleman, I will.*

LEONATO: *Brother Anthony—*

ANTONIO: *Keep calm. What, man! I know them, yes, and what they weigh, even to the smallest measure—quarrelsome, impudent, fashion-conscious boys, who lie and cheat, and jeer, defame and slander, dress fantastically, showing outward such frightening appearance, and spout off a half dozen brave words of how they would hurt their enemies if they choose; and that is all.*

LEONATO: *But, brother Anthony—*

ANTONIO: *Come, it doesn't matter. Don't meddle; let me handle this.*

173

DON PEDRO: Gentlemen both, we will not wake your patience.
My heart is sorry for your daughter's death;
But, on my honour, she was charged with nothing
115   But what was true, and very full of proof.

LEONATO: My lord, my lord—

DON PEDRO: I will not hear you.

LEONATO: No? Come, brother, away!—I will be heard.

ANTONIO: And shall, or some of us will smart for it.

[Enter Benedick.]

120   DON PEDRO: See, see! Here comes the man we went to seek.

CLAUDIO: Now, signior, what news?

BENEDICK: Good day, my lord.

DON PEDRO: Welcome, signior. You are almost come to part almost
a fray.

125   CLAUDIO: We had liked to have had our two noses snapped off with
two old men without teeth.

DON PEDRO: Leonato and his brother. What think'st thou? Had we
fought, I doubt we should have been too young for them.

BENEDICK: In a false quarrel there is no true valour. I came to seek
130   you both.

DON PEDRO: *Please gentlemen, we will not cause you to need patience. My heart is truly sorry for your daughter's death; but on my honor, she was charged only with what was true, and that was fully proved.*

LEONATO: *My lord, my lord—*

DON PEDRO: *I will not hear you.*

LEONATO: *No? Come brother, let's go! I will be heard.*

ANTONIO: *You shall be heard, or someone will answer for it.*

[Enter Benedick.]

DON PEDRO: *See, see! Here comes the man we went to seek.*

CLAUDIO: *Hello, sir, what news?*

BENEDICK: *Good day, my lord.*

DON PEDRO: *Welcome, sir. You almost came in time to stop a fight.*

CLAUDIO: *We almost had our noses snapped off by two old men without teeth.*

DON PEDRO: *Leonato and his brother. What do you think about that? If we had fought, I doubt that we would have been too young for them.*

BENEDICK: *In a false quarrel there is no true bravery. I came to find the both of you.*

CLAUDIO: We have been up and down to seek thee; for we are high-proof melancholy, and would fain have it beaten away. Wilt thou use thy wit?

BENEDICK: It is in my scabbard. Shall I draw it?

135 DON PEDRO: Dost thou wear thy wit by thy side?

CLAUDIO: Never any did so, though very many have been beside their wit. I will bid thee draw, as we do the minstrel—draw to pleasure us.

DON PEDRO: As I am an honest man, he looks pale. Art thou sick or
140   angry?

CLAUDIO: What, courage, man! What though care killed a cat, thou hast mettle enough in thee to kill care.

BENEDICK: Sir, I shall meet your wit in the career an you charge it against me. I pray you choose another subject.

145 CLAUDIO: Nay then, give him another staff; this last was broke cross.

DON PEDRO: By this light, he changes more and more. I think he be angry indeed.

CLAUDIO: If he be, he knows how to turn his girdle.

150 BENEDICK: Shall I speak a word in your ear?

CLAUDIO: God bless me from a challenge!

BENEDICK: [Aside to Claudio] You are a villain. I jest not; I will make it good how you dare, with what you dare, and when

CLAUDIO: We have searched high and low for you; for we are in a high state of depression and wish to have it beaten away. Will you use your humor?

BENEDICK: It is in my scabbard. Shall I draw my sword?

DON PEDRO: Do you wear your wit by your side?

CLAUDIO: No one ever did that, although many have been beside their wits. I ask you to draw as musicians do—draw to please us.

DON PEDRO: As I am an honest man, he looks pale. Are you sick or angry?

CLAUDIO: Well, be strong, man! Although care killed a cat, you have enough strength in you to kill care.

BENEDICK: Sir, I will meet your fast-moving humor if you charge me with it. Please, choose another subject.

CLAUDIO: No, give him another weapon, for this last one was broken across its middle.

DON PEDRO: By this light, he changes more and more. I really think he is angry.

CLAUDIO: If he is, he knows how to wear clothes for fighting.

BENEDICK: May I speak a word in your ear?

CLAUDIO: God save me from a challenge!

BENEDICK: [Aside to Claudio] You are a villain. I'm not joking; I'll prove it to you however you choose, with whatever you

155 you dare. Do me right, or I will protest your cowardice. You have killed a sweet lady, and her death shall fall heavy on you. Let me hear from you.

Claudio: Well, I will meet you, so I may have good cheer.

Don Pedro: What, a feast, a feast?

Claudio: I' faith, I thank him, he hath bid me to a calve's head and 160 a capon, the which if I do not carve most curiously, say my knife's naught. Shall I not find a woodcock too?

Benedick: Sir, your wit ambles well; it goes easily.

Don Pedro: I'll tell thee how Beatrice praised thy wit the other day. I said thou hadst a fine wit: 'True,' said she, 'a fine little one.' 165 'No,' said I, 'a great wit.' 'Right,' says she, 'a great gross one.' 'Nay,' said I, 'a good wit.' 'Just,' said she, 'it hurts nobody.' 'Nay,' said I, 'the gentleman is wise.' 'Certain,' said she, a wise gentleman.' 'Nay,' said I, 'he hath the tongues.' 'That I believe' said she, 'for he swore a thing to me on Monday night which 170 he forswore on Tuesday morning. There's a double tongue; there's two tongues.' Thus did she an hour together trans-shape thy particular virtues. Yet at last she concluded with a sigh, thou wast the properest man in Italy.

Claudio: For the which she wept heartily and said she cared not.

175 Don Pedro: Yea, that she did; but yet, for all that, an if she did not hate him deadly, she would love him dearly. The old man's daughter told us all.

Claudio: All, all! and moreover, God saw him when he was hid in the garden.

178

choose, and whenever you choose. Accept my challenge, or I will report your cowardice. You have killed a sweet lady, and her death will weigh heavily upon you. What do you say to that?

CLAUDIO: *Well, I will meet you, so that I may have some fun.*

DON PEDRO: *What, a feast, a feast?*

CLAUDIO: *Indeed, I thank him, for he has invited me to a fool's feast where I must carve carefully or my knife will be good for nothing. Shouldn't I find a dumb dodo, too?*

BENEDICK: *Sir, your mind flows well, it leaves easily.*

DON PEDRO: *Let me tell you how Beatrice appraised your mind the other day. I said you had a fine mind. "True," she said, "a fine tiny one." "No," said I, "a large mind." "Right." she said, "a big, gross one." "No," said I, "the man is smart." "Agreed," said she, "a smart ass." "No," said I, "he speaks many languages." "I believe it," said she, "since he swore something to me on Monday night which he denied on Tuesday morning. That's using two languages." She thus talked about your virtues for an hour. She stopped at last with a sigh, that you were the handsomest man in Italy.*

CLAUDIO: *And for that she wept mightily and said she didn't care.*

DON PEDRO: *Yes, that's what she did, but for all of that, if she didn't hate him so completely, she would love him dearly. The old man's daughter told us everything.*

CLAUDIO: *Everything, everything! And besides, God saw him when he was hidden in the garden.*

180   DON PEDRO: But when shall we set the savage bull's horns on the sensible Benedick's head?

CLAUDIO: Yea, and text underneath, 'Here dwells Benedick, the married man'?

BENEDICK: Fare you well, boy; you know my mind. I will leave you
185   now to your gossiplike humour. You break jests as braggards do their blades, which God be thanked hurt not. My lord, for your many courtesies I thank you. I must discontinue your company. Your brother the bastard is fled from Messina. You have among you killed a sweet and innocent lady. For my
190   Lord Lackbeard there, he and I shall meet; and till then peace be with him.

[Exit.]

DON PEDRO: He is in earnest.

CLAUDIO: In most profound earnest; and, I'll warrant you, for the love of Beatrice.

195   DON PEDRO: And hath challenged thee.

CLAUDIO: Most sincerely.

DON PEDRO: What a pretty thing man is when he goes in his doublet and hose and leaves off his wit!

CLAUDIO: He is then a giant to an ape; but then is an ape a doctor to
200   such a man.

DON PEDRO: But, soft you, let me be! Pluck up, my heart, and be sad! Did he not say my brother was fled?

DON PEDRO: But when shall we put those horns on the head of the most sensible Benedick?

CLAUDIO: Yes, and put in capital letters underneath, "Here lives Benedick, the married man"?

BENEDICK: Good-by, boy; you know my mind. I'll leave you to your immature fun. You break jokes like cowards do their blades, which, thank God, do not injure. Lord, for your many courtesies, I thank you. But, I must discontinue your fellowship. Your bastard brother has fled Messina. Between you, you have killed a sweet and innocent lady. For Lord Sissy there, he and I shall meet; until then, peace be with him.

[Exit.]

DON PEDRO: He is in earnest.

CLAUDIO: In most profound earnest; and I'll warrant you he did this because of his love of Beatrice.

DON PEDRO: And he has challenged you.

CLAUDIO: Indeed he has.

DON PEDRO: What a strange thing man is when he is fully dressed but forgets to add his sense.

CLAUDIO: Without his sense he is like a giant to an ape, but then an ape can cure such a man.

DON PEDRO: But, calm down. Leave me be! Pull together my heart and be serious. Did he not say that my brother has fled?

[Enter Dogberry, and Verges, with the Watch, leading Conrade and Borachio.]

DOGBERRY: Come you, sir. If justice cannot tame you, she shall ne'er weigh more reasons in her balance. Nay, an you be a cursing
205   hypocrite once, you must be looked to.

DON PEDRO: How now? two of my brother's men bound? Borachio one.

CLAUDIO: Hearken after their offence, my lord.

DON PEDRO: Officers, what offence have these men done?

210 DOGBERRY: Marry, sir, they have committed false report; moreover, they have spoken untruths; secondarily, they are slanders; sixth and lastly, they have belied a lady; thirdly, they have verified unjust things; and to conclude, they are lying knaves.

DON PEDRO: First, I ask thee what they have done; thirdly, I ask
215   thee what's their offence; sixth and lastly, why they are committed; and to conclude, what you lay to their charge?

CLAUDIO: Rightly reasoned, and in his own division; and by my troth there's one meaning well suited.

DON PEDRO: Who have you offended, masters, that you are thus
220   bound to your answer? This learned constable is too cunning to be understood. What's your offence?

BORACHIO: Sweet prince, let me go no farther to mine answer. Do you hear me, and let this count kill me. I have deceived even your very eyes. What your wisdoms could not discover, these
225   shallow fools have brought to light, who in the night

[Enter Dogberry and Verges, with the Watch, leading Conrade and Borachio.]

DOGBERRY: Come, sir. If justice cannot tame you, then she shall never weigh more reasons in her scales. And even though you are a foul-mouthed hypocrite, you must be looked after.

DON PEDRO: What's this? Two of my brother's men bound with ropes? One is Borachio.

CLAUDIO: Ask what they have done, my lord.

DON PEDRO: Officers, what crime have these men committed?

DOGBERRY: Well, sir, they have given false reports; also, they have spoken non-truths; secondly, they are slanderers, sixth and lastly, they have lied about a lady; thirdly, they have verified untruths, and to conclude, they are lying knaves.

DON PEDRO: First, I ask you what they have done; thirdly, I ask you what is their crime; sixth and lastly, why they are arrested; and to conclude, what do you charge them with?

CLAUDIO: Rightly reasoned, and in his own fashion; and believe me, that's one meaning provided with several different interpretations.

DON PEDRO: Who have you offended, sirs, that you are bound up so? This learned constable is too cunning to be understood. What's your crime?

BORACHIO: Dear prince, let me answer quickly. Please hear me, and then let this count kill me. I have deceived your own eyes. What your intelligence could not discover, these idiots have brought to light by hearing me confess to this man how

overheard me confessing to this man, how Don John your
brother incensed me to slander the Lady Hero; how you were
brought into the orchard and saw me court Margaret in Hero's
garments; how you disgraced her when you should marry her.
230 My villany they have upon record, which I had rather seal
with my death than repeat over to my shame. The lady is dead
upon mine and my master's false accusation; and briefly, I
desire nothing but the reward of a villain.

DON PEDRO: Runs not this speech like iron through your blood?

235 CLAUDIO: I have drunk poison whiles he uttered it.

DON PEDRO: But did my brother set thee on to this?

BORACHIO: Yea, and paid me richly for the practice of it.

DON PEDRO: He is composed and framed of treachery,
And fled he is upon this villany.

240 CLAUDIO: Sweet Hero, now thy image doth appear
In the rare semblance that I loved it first.

DOGBERRY: Come, bring away the plaintiffs. By this time our sexton
hath reformed Signior Leonato of the matter. And, masters, do
not forget to specify, when time and place shall serve, that I
am an ass.

245 VERGES: Here, here comes Master Signior Leonato, and the sexton
too.

your brother, Don John, incited me to slander Lady Hero;
how you were led to the orchard and saw me court Margaret
dressed in Hero's clothes; how you disgraced her when you
should have married her. My crimes are written down which
I would rather seal with my death than repeat. The lady is
dead because of my and my master's lies; and briefly, I want
nothing but the reward of a villain.

DON PEDRO: *Doesn't this speech run through your blood like a*
sword?

CLAUDIO: *I felt ill while he spoke it.*

DON PEDRO: *Did my brother put you up to this?*

BORACHIO: *Yes, and paid me very well for its completion.*

DON PEDRO: *He is filled with this treachery, and has fled because*
of it.

CLAUDIO: *Sweet Hero, now your image appears in the rare form I*
first loved.

DOGBERRY: *Come, bring away the plaintiffs¹. By this time our sex-*
ton has reformed² Leonato of this matter. And, sirs, do not
forget to specify, when the time and place is proper, that I
am an ass.

VERGES: *Here, here comes Master Signior Leonato and the sexton.*

---

1.   plaintiffs - defendants
2.   reformed - informed

[Enter Leonato, his brother, Antonio, and the sexton.]

Leonato: Which is the villain? Let me see his eyes,
      That, when I note another man like him,
      I may avoid him. Which of these is he?

250 Borachio: If you would know your wronger, look on me.

Leonato: Art thou the slave that with thy breath hast killed
      Mine innocent child?

Borachio: Yea, even I alone.

Leonato: No, not so, villain! thou beliest thyself.
255   Here stand a pair of honourable men—
      A third is fled—that had a hand in it.
      I thank you princes for my daughter's death.
      Record it with your high and worthy deeds.
      Twas bravely done, if you bethink you of it.

260 Claudio: I know not how to pray your patience;
      Yet I must speak. Choose your revenge yourself;
      Impose me to what penance your invention
      Can lay upon my sin. Yet sinned I not
      But in mistaking.

265 Don Pedro: By my soul, nor I!
      And yet, to satisfy this good old man,
      I would bend under any heavy weight
      That he'll enjoin me to.

Leonato: I cannot bid you bid my daughter live;
270   That were impossible; but I pray you both,
      Possess the people in Messina here
      How innocent she died; and if your love
      Can labour aught in sad invention,
      Hang her an epitaph upon her tomb,

[Enter Leonato, his brother Antonio, and the sexton.]

LEONATO: Which one is the villain? Let me see his eyes that when I see another man like him, I may avoid him. Which of these men is he?

BORACHIO: If you would know the culprit, look on me.

LEONATO: Are you the scum whose lies have killed my innocent child?

BORACHIO: Yes, I alone did it.

LEONATO: No, not true, villain. You are lying. Here stand two honorable men—a third has fled—who have a hand in this. I thank you princes for my daughter's death. Record it with your high and worthy deeds. It was so bravely done, if you think about it.

CLAUDIO: I don't know how to ask your forgiveness, yet I must speak. Choose your own revenge; impose on me whatever penance your imagination can lay upon my sin. Yet I sinned not, but in mistaking the appearance for reality.

DON PEDRO: By my soul, nor I! Yet; to satisfy this goodly old man, I would bend under any heavy charge that he would impose on me.

LEONATO: I cannot have you bid life to my daughter, that is impossible. However, I ask both of you to inform the people of Messina of my daughter's innocence. If your feelings are sober and serious, hang an epitaph on her tomb and sing it to her remains—sing it tonight. Tomorrow, come to my

275   And sing it to her bones—sing it to-night.
       To-morrow morning come you to my house,
       And since you could not be my son-in-law,
       Be yet my nephew. My brother hath a daughter,
       Almost the copy of my child that's dead,
280   And she alone is heir to both of us.
       Give her the right you should have giv'n her cousin,
       And so dies my revenge.

CLAUDIO: O noble sir!
       Your over-kindness doth wring tears from me.
285   I do embrace your offer; and dispose
       For henceforth of poor Claudio.

LEONATO: To-morrow then I will expect your coming;
       To-night I take my leave. This naughty man
       Shall face to face be brought to Margaret,
290   Who I believe was packed in all this wrong,
       Hired to it by your brother.

BORACHIO: No, by my soul, she was not;
       Nor knew not what she did when she spoke to me;
       But always hath been just and virtuous
295   In anything that I do know by her.

DOGBERRY: Moreover, my lord, which indeed is not under white
       and black, this plaintiff here, the offender, did call me ass.
       I beseech you let it be remembered in his punishment. And
       also the watch heard them talk of one Deformed. They say
300   he wears a key in his ear, and a lock hanging by it, and bor-
       rows money in God's name, the which he hath used so long
       and never paid that now men grow hard-hearted and will
       lend nothing for God's sake. Pray you examine him upon that
       point.

305   LEONATO: I thank thee for thy care and honest pains.

house, and since you could not be my son-in-law, then be my nephew. My brother has a daughter, almost a duplicate of my dead child, and she alone is heir to both of us. Give her the respect you should have given her cousin. Do this and my revenge dies.

CLAUDIO: Oh, noble sir! Your magnanimous gesture wrings tears from me. I do embrace your offer, and you can dispose immediately of poor Claudio.

LEONATO: Tomorrow I will expect you; tonight I leave you. [Facing Borachio] This awful man will be brought face to face with Margaret, who I believe was an accessory to the crime, hired by your brother to do it.

BORACHIO: No, by my soul, she was not; nor did she know anything of what she did when she spoke to me; she has always been honest and virtuous in everything I have known her to do.

DOGBERRY: Also, my lord, while not written down, this plaintiff here, the offender, did call me "ass." Please let it be remembered in his punishment. The watch also heard them talk of one Deformed. They say he wears a key in his ear with a lock hanging from it, and borrows money in the name of God so often without repayment that men will no longer lend God money. Ask him about that.

LEONATO: Thank you for your hard work and honest labor.

DogBerry: Your worship speaks like a most thankful and reverent youth, and I praise God for you.

Leonato: There's for thy pains. [Gives money.]

DogBerry: God save the foundation!

310   Leonato: Go, I discharge thee of thy prisoner, and I thank thee.

DogBerry: I leave an arrant knave with your worship, which I beseech your worship to correct yourself, for the example of others. God keep your worship! I wish your worship well. God restore you to health! I humbly give you leave to depart;
315   and if a merry meeting may be wished, God prohibit it! Come neighbour.

[Exeunt Dogberry and Verges.]

Leonato: Until to-morrow morning, lords, farewell.

Antonio: Farewell, my lords. We look for you to-morrow.

Don Pedro: We will not fail.

320   Claudio: To-night I'll mourn with Hero.

[Exeunt Don Pedro and Claudio.]

Leonato: [To the Watch]
Bring you these fellows on.–We'll talk with Margaret,
How her acquaintance grew with this lewd fellow.

[Exeunt.]

DOGBERRY: *Your worship speaks like a most thankful and reverent youth, and I praise God for you.*

LEONATO: *Here's for your trouble. [Gives him money.]*

DOGBERRY: *God save the foundation!*

LEONATO: *Go, I'll take charge of your prisoner, and I thank you again.*

DOGBERRY: *I leave a simple knave with your worship, who I beseech your worship to correct yourself, for others' example. God keep your worship! I wish your worship well. God restore you to health—I humbly give you leave to depart; and if we should have a happy reunion, may God prohibit it. Come, neighbor.*

[Exit Dogberry and Verges.]

LEONATO: *Until tomorrow, lords, farewell.*

ANTONIO: *Farewell, my lords. We'll look to see you tomorrow.*

DON PEDRO: *We will not fail you.*

CLAUDIO: *Tonight I will mourn with Hero.*

[Exit Don Pedro and Claudio.]

LEONATO: *[To the Watch] Bring these men along. We'll talk with Margaret about her relationship with this disreputable fellow.*

[Exit]

Scene 2
Leonato's Garden

[Enter Benedick and Margaret, meeting.]

BENEDICK: Pray thee, sweet Mistress Margaret, deserve well at my
hands by helping me to the speech of Beatrice.

MARGARET: Will you then write me a sonnet in praise of my
beauty?

5   BENEDICK: In so high a style, Margaret, that no man living shall
come over it; for in most comely truth thou deservest it.

MARGARET: To have no man come over me? Why, shall I always
keep below stairs?

BENEDICK: Thy wit is as quick as the greyhound's mouth—it
10   catches.

MARGARET: And yours as blunt as the fencer's foils, which hit but
hurt not.

BENEDICK: A most manly wit, Margaret; it will not hurt a woman.
And so I pray thee call Beatrice. I give thee the bucklers.

15   MARGARET: Give us the swords; we have bucklers of our own.

BENEDICK: If you use them, Margaret, you must put in the pikes
with a vice, and they are dangerous weapons for maids.

MARGARET: Well, I will call Beatrice to you, who I think hath legs.

BENEDICK: And therefore will come.
                                        [Exit Margaret.]

Scene 2
Leonato's Garden

[Enter Benedick and Margaret, meeting.]

BENEDICK: Please, mistress Margaret, win my gratitude by helping me write a poem about Beatrice.

MARGARET: Will you then write me a sonnet praising my beauty?

BENEDICK: In such high style, Margaret, that no living man will come over you; for, in truth, you deserve that.

MARGARET: To have no man come over me? Why, shall I always be a servant?

BENEDICK: Your wit is as quick as a greyhound's mouth—it does catch the prey.

MARGARET: And yours is as dull as a fencer's practice weapon which hits but doesn't hurt.

BENEDICK: A most manly mind, Margaret; it wouldn't hurt a woman. So turn ideas to Beatrice; I'll give you shields to protect yourself.

MARGARET: Give us the swords, we have shields of our own.

BENEDICK: If you use them, Margaret, you must turn the spikes with a screw, and they are dangerous weapons for girls.

MARGARET: Well, I'll fetch Beatrice to you who I think has legs.

BENEDICK: And therefore will come.

[Exit Margaret.]

20   [Sings] The god of love,
                        That sits above
                        And knows me, and knows me,
                        How pitiful I deserve—
        I mean in singing; but in loving Leander the good swim-
25   mer, Troilus the first employer of panders, and a whole book
        full of these quondam carpet-mongers, whose names yet run
        smoothly in the even road of a blank verse—why, they were
        never so truly turned over and over as my poor self in love.
        Marry, I cannot show it in rhyme. I have tried. I can find out
30   no rhyme to 'lady' but 'baby'—an innocent rhyme; for 'scorn,'
        'horn'—a hard rhyme; for school', 'fool'—a babbling rhyme:
        very ominous endings! No, I was not born under a rhyming
        planet, nor cannot woo in festival terms. [Enter Beatrice.]
        Sweet Beatrice, wouldst thou come when I called thee?

35   BEATRICE: Yea, signior, and depart when you bid me.

     BENEDICK: O, stay but till then!

     BEATRICE: 'Then' is spoken. Fare you well now. And yet, ere I go, let
        me go with that I came for, which is, with knowing what hath
        passed between you and Claudio.

40   BENEDICK: Only foul words; and thereupon I will kiss thee.

     BEATRICE: Foul words is but foul wind, and foul wind is but foul
        breath, and foul breath is noisome. Therefore I will depart
        unkissed.

     BENEDICK: Thou hast frighted the word out of his right sense, so
45   forcible is thy wit. But I must tell thee plainly, Claudio under-
        goes my challenge; and either I must shortly hear from him
        or I will subscribe him a coward. And I pray thee now tell
        me, for which of my bad parts didst thou first fall in love with
        me?

[Sings] *The god of love,*
>   *That sits above*
>   *And knows me, and knows me,*
>   *How pitiful I deserve—*

I mean in singing; but in loving neither Leander the good swimmer, Troilus the first employer of pimps, nor a whole book full of carpet-knights whose names run smoothly in poems, were ever so truly so head over heels in love. But I can't say it in rhyme, I have tried. I can find no rhyme to "lady" but "baby" —an innocent rhyme; for "scorn," "horn" a hard rhyme; for "school," "fool"—a babbling rhyme. Very strange endings! No, I wasn't born under a rhyming planet, and I cannot woo in festive words. *[Enter Beatrice.]* Sweet Beatrice, would you come when I call you?

BEATRICE: Yes, Signior, and depart when you tell me.

BENEDICK: Well, stay until then!

BEATRICE: "Then" is spoken. Good-bye. Yet before I leave let me have what I came for, which is to know what words were exchanged between you and Claudio.

BENEDICK: Only foul words, and now I will kiss you.

BEATRICE: Foul words are foul wind, and foul wind is bad-smelling and foul breath is very offensive. Therefore, I will leave unkissed.

BENEDICK: You have scared the word right out of its proper meaning so strong is your wit. But I must tell you honestly that Claudio has my challenge, and either I must hear from him shortly or I will call him down a coward. But please tell me now, for which of my bad parts did you first fall in love with me?

50 BEATRICE: For them all together, which maintained so politic a state
of evil that they will not admit any good part to intermingle
with them. But for which of my good parts did you first suffer
love for me?

BENEDICK: Suffer love!—a good epithet. I do suffer love indeed, for I
55 love thee against my will.

BEATRICE: In spite of your heart, I think. Alas, poor heart! If you
spite it for my sake, I will spite it for yours, for I will never
love that which my friend hates.

BENEDICK: Thou and I are too wise to woo peaceably.

60 BEATRICE: It appears not in this confession. There's not one wise
man among twenty, that will praise himself.

BENEDICK: An old, an old instance, Beatrice, that lived in the time
of good neighbours. If a man do not erect in this age his own
tomb ere he dies, he shall live no longer in monument than
65 the bell rings and the widow weeps.

BEATRICE: And how long is that, think you?

BENEDICK: Question: why, an hour in clamour and a quarter in
rheum. Therefore is it most expedient for the wise, if Don
Worm, his conscience find no impediment to the contrary, to
70 be the trumpet of his own virtues, as I am to myself. So much
for praising myself, who, I myself will bear witness, is praiseworthy. And now tell me, how doth your cousin?

BEATRICE: Very ill.

BENEDICK: And how do you?

196

BEATRICE: *For all of them together, which were so evil and well organized that they wouldn't allow any good parts to mingle with them. But for which of my good parts did you first suffer love for me?*

BENEDICK: *Suffer love!—a good phrase. I really do suffer love, for I love you against my will.*

BEATRICE: *Despite your heart, I think. Ah, poor heart. If you spite it for my sake, I will spite it for yours, for I would never love anything that my friend hates.*

BENEDICK: *You and I are too wise to woo peacefully.*

BEATRICE: *The answer isn't in your confession. There's not one wise man in twenty who would praise himself.*

BENEDICK: *An old, old saying, Beatrice, that lived back in the Golden Ages. If a man does not build his own tomb when he lives, his memory shall live on no longer than the bell rings or the widow weeps.*

BEATRICE: *And how long do you think that is?*

BENEDICK: *Question: why, an hour in commotion and three months in tears. Therefore, it is best for the wise, if his conscience doesn't stop him, to trumpet his own virtues as I do. As to praising myself: I have to honestly say I am praiseworthy. And now tell me, how is Hero?*

BEATRICE: *Very ill.*

BENEDICK: *And how are you?*

75   BEATRICE: Very ill too.

BENEDICK: Serve God, love me, and mend. There will I leave you
too, for here comes one in haste.

URSULA: Madam, you must come to your uncle. Yonder's old coil
at home. It is proved my Lady Hero hath been falsely accused
80   the prince and Claudio mightily abused, and Don John is the
author of all, who is fled and gone. Will you come presently?

BEATRICE: Will you go hear this news, signior?

BENEDICK: I will live in thy heart, die in thy lap, and be buried in
thy eyes; and moreover, I will go with thee to thy uncle's.

[Exeunt.]

Scene 3
The Inside of a Church

[Enter Don Pedro, Claudio, and Attendants, with music and candles.]

CLAUDIO: Is this the monument of Leonato?

LORD: It is, my lord.

CLAUDIO: [reads from a scroll]

Epitaph.
Done to death by slanderous tongues
5   Was the Hero that here lies.
Death, in guerdon of her wrongs,

BEATRICE: *Very ill, too.*

BENEDICK: *Serve God, love me, and mend. But I must go becuase someone comes in haste.*

URSULA: *Madam, you must come to your uncle. The confusion has come home. It has been proved that Hero was falsely accused, the prince and Claudio mightily deceived, and Don John, the instigator of this, has fled. Will you come now?*

BEATRICE: *Signior, will you also go to hear this news?*

BENEDICK: *I will live in your heart, die in your lap, and be buried in your eyes. Further, I will go with you to your uncle's.*

[Exit.]

Scene 3
The Inside of a Church

[Enter Don Pedro, Claudio, and Attendants, with music and candles.]

CLAUDIO: *Is this the family tomb of Leonato?*

LORD: *It is, my lord.*

CLAUDIO: *[reads from a scroll]*

Epitaph.
Done to death by slanderous tongues
Was the Hero that lies here.
Death, in reward of her wrongs,

Gives her fame which never dies.
So the life that died with shame
Lives in death with glorious fame.

[Hanging up the scroll.]
10 Hang thou there upon the tomb,
Praising her when I am dumb.
Now, music, sound, and sing your solemn hymn.

[Song.]

Pardon, goddess of the night,
Those that slew thy virgin knight;
15 For the which, with songs of woe,
Round about her tomb they go.
Midnight, assist our moan,
Help us to sigh and groan
Heavily, heavily,
20 Graves, yawn and yield your dead,
Till death be uttered
Heavily, heavily.

CLAUDIO: Now unto thy bones good night!
 Yearly will I do this rite.

25 DON PEDRO: Good morrow, masters. Put your torches out.
 The wolves have preyed, and look, the gentle day,
 Before the wheels of Phoebus, round about
 Dapples the drowsy east with spots of grey.
 Thanks to you all, and leave us. Fare you well.

30 CLAUDIO: Good morrow, masters. Each his several way.

DON PEDRO: Come, let us hence and put on other weeds,
 And then to Leonato's we will go.

Gives her fame which never dies.
So the life that died with shame
Lives in death with glorious fame.

[He hangs up the scroll].
Hang upon the tomb, to praise
her when I am dumb.
Now, music sound, and sing your solemn hymn.

[One attendant sings:]

Pardon, goddess of the night,
Those that slew thy virgin knight;
For the which, with songs of woe,
Round about her tomb they go.
Midnight, assist our moan,
Help us to sigh and groan
Heavily, heavily.
Graves, yawn and yield your dead,
Till death be uttered
Heavily, heavily.

CLAUDIO: Now unto your bones good night. I will do this ritual yearly.

DON PEDRO: Good day, sirs. Put your torches out. Night has passed and the wheels of the sun colors the sleepy East with light clouds. Thank you all and leave us. Farewell.

CLAUDIO: Good-bye, gentlemen. Each to your own way.

DON PEDRO: Come, let us go and put on other clothes and then to Leonato's we will go.

CLAUDIO: And Hymen now with luckier issue speeds Than this for whom we rendered up this woe.

Scene 4
A Room in Leonato's House

[Enter Leonato, Benedick, Beatrice, Margaret, Ursula, Antonio, Friar Francis and Hero.]

FRIAR: Did I not tell you she was innocent?

LEONATO: So are the prince and Claudio, who accused her
Upon the error that you heard debated.
But Margaret was in some fault for this,
5   Although against her will, as it appears
In the true course of all the question.

ANTONIO: Well, I am glad that all things sort so well

BENEDICK: And so am I, being else by faith enforced To call young Claudio to a reckoning for it.

10 LEONATO: Well, daughter, and you gentlewomen all,
Withdraw into a chamber by yourselves,
And when I send for you, come hither masked.
The prince and Claudio promised by this hour
To visit me. You know your office, brother:
15   You must be father to your brother's daughter,
And give her to young Claudio.

[Exeunt Ladies.]

ANTONIO: Which I will do with confirmed countenance.

202

CLAUDIO: And marriage now comes with luckier speed than it did for the one we have rendered this woe.

Scene 4
A Room in Leonato's House

[Enter Leonato, Benedick, Beatrice, Margaret, Ursula, Antonio, Friar Francis and Hero.]

FRIAR: Didn't I tell you she was innocent?

LEONATO: So are the prince and Claudio, who had accused her because of the facts you have heard debated. But Margaret was somewhat at fault in this, although it appears it was against her will according to the investigation.

ANTONIO: Well, I am glad everything is sorted out so well.

BENEDICK: So am I; otherwise, I'd have to call Claudio to terms for it.

LEONATO: My daughter and you gentlewomen, go to your chambers alone. When I send for you, return with masks on. The prince and Claudio have promised to visit me this very hour. Brother, you know your part; you must be the father to your brother's daughter and give her to young Claudio.

[Exit Ladies.]

ANTONIO: Which I will do with a straight face.

BENEDICK: Friar, I must entreat your pains, I think.

FRIAR: To do what, signior?

20 BENEDICK: To bind me, or undo me—one of them.
       Signior Leonato, truth it is, good signior,
       Your niece regards me with an eye of favour.

LEONATO: That eye my daughter lent her. 'Tis most true.

BENEDICK: And I do with an eye of love requite her.

25 LEONATO: The sight whereof I think you had from me,
       From Claudio, and the prince; but what's your will?

BENEDICK: Your answer, my lord, is enigmatical;
       But, for my will, my will is, your good will
       May stand with ours, this day to be conjoined
30   In the state of honourable marriage;
       In which, good friar, I shall desire your help.

LEONATO: My heart is with your liking.

FRIAR: And my help. Here comes the prince and Claudio.

[Enter Don Pedro and Claudio and two or three other.]

DON PEDRO: Good morrow to this fair assembly.

35 LEONATO: Good morrow, prince; good morrow, Claudio.
       We here attend you. Are you yet determined
       To-day to marry with my brother's daughter?

CLAUDIO: I'll hold my mind, were she an Ethiope.

LEONATO: Call her forth, brother. Here's the friar ready.
                                          [Exit Antonio.]

204

BENEDICK: *Friar, I must seek your assistance, I think.*

FRIAR: *To do what, signior?*

BENEDICK: *To either bind me or undo me. Signior Leonato, the truth is that your niece looks favorably upon.*

LEONATO: *My daughter helped form that opinion. That's most true.*

BENEDICK: *And I with an eye of love return her love.*

LEONATO: *Your eyes, I think, were focused by me, by Claudio, and by the prince. But, what do you want?*

BENEDICK: *Your answer, sir, is puzzling; but, for my will, my will is that your good will might join with ours; that this day to be joined in the state of matrimony. In which, good friar, I shall desire your help.*

LEONATO: *My heart feels the same way.*

FRIAR: *And I will give my help. Here comes the prince and Claudio.*

[Enter Don Pedro, Claudio and two or three others.]

DON PEDRO: *Good morning to the wonderful gathering.*

LEONATO: *Good morning, prince; good morning, Claudio. We are here to serve you. Are you still determined to wed my niece today?*

CLAUDIO: *I'd do it even if she were an Ethiopian.*

LEONATO: *Call her here, brother. The friar is ready.*
                                    [Exit Antonio.]

40 DON PEDRO: Good morrow, Benedick. Why, what's the matter
        That you have such a February face,
        So full of frost, of storm, and cloudiness?

    CLAUDIO: I think he thinks upon the savage bull.
        Tush, fear not, man! We'll tip thy horns with gold,
45   And all Europa shall rejoice at thee,
        As once Europa did at lusty Jove
        When he would play the noble beast in love.

    BENEDICK: Bull Jove, my lord, had an amiable low,
        And some such strange bull leaped your father's cow
50   And got a calf in that same noble feat.
        Much like to you, for you have just his bleat.

    CLAUDIO: For this I owe you. [Enter Leonato's brother, Antonio,
        Hero, Beatrice, Margaret, Ursula, the ladies wearing masks].
        Here comes other reckonings. Which is the lady I must seize
55   upon?

    ANTONIO: This same is she, and I do give you her.

    CLAUDIO: Why then, she's mine. Sweet, let me see your face.

    LEONATO: No, that you shall not till you take her hand
        Before this friar and swear to marry her.

60 CLAUDIO: Give me your hand before this holy friar. I am your hus-
        band if you like of me.

    HERO: And when I lived I was your other wife; [Unmasks.] And
        when you loved you were my other husband.

    CLAUDIO: Another Hero!

DON PEDRO: *Good morning, Benedick. Why, what's the matter that you have such a cold face, full of frost, of storm, and cloudiness.*

CLAUDIO: *I believe he thinks about the savage bull. There, there, man, don't be afraid. We'll tip your horn with gifts of gold and all of Europe will rejoice with you as Europe did when the god Jove appeared as a lustful bull.*

BENEDICK: *Bull Jove, my lord, had a pleasant call, but some strange bull must have leapt upon your father's cow and conceived a calf similar to you, for you have the same bleat.*

CLAUDIO: *I owe you one for this. [Enter Antonio, Hero, Beatrice, Margaret and* URSULA: *The ladies are wearing masks]. But here comes other matters. Which one is the lady I must take in hand?*

ANTONIO: *This is she, and I do give her to you.*

CLAUDIO: *Why then, she's mine. Sweet lady, let me see your face.*

LEONATO: *No. You can't do that until you take her hand before this priest and swear to marry her.*

CLAUDIO: *Give me your hand before this holy friar. I am be your husband if you want me.*

HERO: *And when I lived, I was your other wife; and when you loved, you were my other husband. [She takes off her mask.]*

CLAUDIO: *Another Hero!*

65 Hero: Nothing certainer.
      One Hero died defiled; but I do live,
      And surely as I live, I am a maid.

Don Pedro: The former Hero! Hero that is dead!

Leonato: She died, my lord, but whiles her slander lived.

70 Friar: All this amazement can I qualify,
      When, after that the holy rites are ended,
      I'll tell you largely of fair Hero's death.
      Meantime let wonder seem familiar,
      And to the chapel let us presently.

75 Benedick: Soft and fair, friar. Which is Beatrice?

Beatrice: [unmasks] I answer to that name. What is your will?

Benedick: Do not you love me?

Beatrice: Why, no; no more than reason.

Benedick: Why, then your uncle, and the prince, and Claudio
80   Have been deceived; for they swore you did.

Beatrice: Do not you love me?

Benedick: Troth, no; no more than reason.

Beatrice: Why, then my cousin, Margaret, and Ursula Are much
      deceived; for they did swear you did.

85 Benedick: They swore that you were almost sick for me.

Beatrice: They swore that you were well-nigh dead for me.

HERO: *Nothing is more certain. One Hero died disgraced, but I do live. And as surely as I live, I am a virgin.*

DON PEDRO: *The former Hero; the Hero that is dead!*

LEONATO: *She died my lord, only while those lies lived.*

FRIAR: *I can enlighten all this confusion after the marriage ceremony is complete by fully explaining fair Hero's death. Meanwhile, treat this wonder as if it were commonplace and let us go to the chapel.*

BENEDICK: *Well put, friar. Which is Beatrice?*

BEATRICE: *[unmasks] I answer to that name. What is your will?*

BENEDICK: *Do you not love me?*

BEATRICE: *Why, no; no more than reason allows.*

BENEDICK: *Why, then your uncle, the prince, and Claudio have been misled, for they swore you did.*

BEATRICE: *Do you not love me?*

BENEDICK: *Honestly, no; no more than reason allows.*

BEATRICE: *Why, then my cousin, Margaret and Ursula have been misled, for they swore you did.*

BENEDICK: *They swore that you were most sick for the love of me.*

BEATRICE: *They swore you were almost dead for me.*

BENEDICK: 'Tis no such matter. Then you do not love me?

BEATRICE: No, truly, but in friendly recompense.

LEONATO: Come, cousin, I am sure you love the gentleman.

90 CLAUDIO: And I'll be sworn upon't that he loves her;
For here's a paper written in his hand,
A halting sonnet of his own pure brain,
Fashioned to Beatrice.

HERO: And here's another,
95 Writ in my cousin's hand, stolen from her pocket,
Containing her affection unto Benedick.

BENEDICK: A miracle! Here's our own hands against our hearts.
Come, I will have thee; but, by this light, I take thee for pity.

BEATRICE: I would not deny you; but, by this good day, I yield upon
100 great persuasion, and partly to save your life, for I was told
you were in a consumption.

BENEDICK: Peace! I will stop your mouth. [Kisses her.]

DON PEDRO: How dost thou, Benedick, the married man?

BENEDICK: I'll tell thee what, prince; a college of wit-crackers can-
105 not flout me out of my humour. Dost thou think I care for a
satire or an epigram? No. If a man will be beaten with brains,
'a shall wear nothing handsome about him. In brief, since I
do purpose to marry, I will think nothing to any purpose that
the world can say against it; and therefore never flout at me
110 for what I have said against it; for man is a giddy thing, and
this is my conclusion. For thy part, Claudio, I did think to
have beaten thee; but in that thou art like to be my kinsman,
live unbruised, and love my cousin.

BENEDICK: *It's not important. Then you don't love me?*

BEATRICE: *Honestly, no—except in charitable friendship.*

LEONATO: *Come on, cousin, I'm sure you love this man.*

CLAUDIO: *And I'll be sworn that he loves her; for here is a paper written by him, a feeble poem fashioned to Beatrice by his own brain.*

HERO: *And here's another written in my cousin's hand, stolen from her pocket, which professes her love of Benedick.*

BENEDICK: *A miracle! Here's written testimony refuting our hearts. Come here, I'll have you. In light of this, I'll take you out of pity.*

BEATRICE: *I would not deny you. Because of this happy day, I'll yield to such persuasion, and partly to save your life for I was told you were near death.*

BENEDICK: *Peace! I'll stop your mouth. [He kisses her.]*

DON PEDRO: *How are you, Benedick, the married man?*

BENEDICK: *I'll tell you what, prince; an assembly of jokers couldn't change my mind. Do you think I mind a joke or two? No. If a man is defeated by wits he has nothing handsome to show for it. Briefly, since I do intend to marry, I will not tolerate anything the world can say against it. Therefore, never jest at me for what I have said against it for man is a silly thing, and that's my conclusion. For your part, Claudio, I would have enjoyed beating you, but since you are likely to be my relative, live on unbruised, and love my cousin.*

CLAUDIO: I had well hoped thou wouldst have denied Beatrice, that
115   I might have cudgelled thee out of thy single life, to make
thee a double-dealer, which out of question thou wilt be if my
cousin do not look exceeding narrowly to thee.

BENEDICK: Come, come, we are friends. Let's have a dance ere we
are married, that we may lighten our own hearts and our
120   wives' heels.

LEONATO: We'll have dancing afterward.

BENEDICK: First, of my word! Therefore play, music. Prince, thou
art sad. Get thee a wife, get thee a wife! There is no staff more
reverent than one tipped with horn.

[Enter Messenger.]

125   MESSENGER: My lord, your brother Don John is taken in flight,
And brought with armed men back to Messina.

BENEDICK: Think not on him till to-morrow. I'll devise thee brave
punishments for him. Strike up, pipers!

[Dance. Exeunt.]

CLAUDIO: I was hoping you would have refused Beatrice so I might have beaten you out of your single life and made you a double-dealer, which certainly you will be unless my cousin pays close attention to you.

BENEDICK: Come, come, we are friends. Let's dance before we are married that we might lighten our own hearts and our wive's heels.

LEONATO: We'll have the dancing afterwards.

BENEDICK: Before, by my word! Play, music. Prince, you look sad. Get a wife, get a wife! There is no job more respectful than marriage.

[Enter Messenger.]

MESSENGER: My lord, your brother Don John has been captured and brought back under guard to Messina.

BENEDICK: Don't think about him until tomorrow. I'll devise you some great punishments for him. Play, pipers.

[They all dance then exit.]

Study Guide

ACT I, Scene 1

1. The messenger tells Leonato, governor of Messina, that the men are returning from battle. What information does the messenger give about Claudio, Benedick and Don Pedro?

2. Why does Leonato feel it necessary to explain to the messenger Beatrice's comments?
   "You must not, sir, mistake my niece. There is a merry war betwixt Signior Benedick and her. They never meet but there's a skirmish of wit between them."

3. How would you describe Beatrice? What feelings about marriage do both Beatrice and Benedick share?

4. What is learned about Don John?

5. What does Claudio ask Benedick?

6. Why does Benedick seem opposed to marriage? When Benedick says he will stay a bachelor, what does Don Pedro predict?

7. One theme of the play is that "things are not as they seem." What action takes place that night which is also not as it seems?

ACT 1, Scene 2

8. What misinformation does Antonio give to his brother? Where has Antonio received this information?

ACT I, Scene 3

9. How does Don John, explain his depression to Conrade?

10. What does Conrade suggest?

11. How does Don John describe himself?

12. Explain Don John's remark about Claudio: "That young start-up hath all the glory of my overthrow."

13. When a bastard half-brother appears in a Shakespearean play, he usually is a resentful, angry villain. Explain how the law of primogeniture in the 16th century might have been a cause of this resentment.

14. How does Don John's personality and behavior contrast with every other character thus far?

ACT II, Scene 1

1. In what way is Beatrice like Benedick? What does Beatrice have against marriage?

2. How does Beatrice insult Benedick? A little later, how does the reader know that Benedick is upset?

3. As the people enter the ballroom, how do they pair off? Don John sees his brother speaking of love to Hero. Then he sees one man with his mask still on, and Borachio tells Don John that the masked man is Claudio. Why does Don John ask Claudio if he is Signior Benedick?

4. When he is alone, what do we see is Claudio's response to the news that Don John has just given him?

5. To what does Benedick compare Claudio? What is being suggested about Claudio?

6.   How does Don Pedro tease Beatrice? What is Don Pedro's
     opinion of Beatrice?

7.   How is Beatrice a foil or a contrast to Don John? How is
     Beatrice a foil for Hero?

8.   The war is over and this happy, harmonious time is celebrat-
     ed with a masquerade ball. In what way is Don John's pres-
     ence an exception to the harmony?

ACT II, Scene 2
9.   Explain Borachio's scheme to end the marriage plans of
     Claudio and Hero? What is Don John's part in the plan?
     According to Borachio, why will Margaret cooperate in this?

ACT II, Scene 3
10. What is the point of Benedick's soliloquy? What does
     Benedick do as Leonato, Claudio, and Don Pedro enter? Why
     does he do this?

11. Describe three things that convince Benedick that these men
     are telling the truth.

12. When Beatrice announces dinner to Benedick, what is
     Benedick's reaction to her comments?

ACT III, Scene 1
1.   What does Hero tell Margaret to do? What does Hero tell
     Ursula to do? To what animal does Hero compare Beatrice?

2.   How much truth is there in Hero's criticism of Beatrice? For
     what reasons does Beatrice decide to return Benedick's love?

ACT III, Scene 2

3.   Describe how Don Pedro and Claudio tease Benedick. Why does Benedick leave with Leonato?

4.   What does Don John mean when he says to Don Pedro and Claudio that Hero is, "Leonato's Hero, your Hero, every man's Hero?" How does he propose to prove this?

5.   Describe how Claudio and Don Pedro respond to Don John's accusations against Hero. What do Claudio and Don Pedro plan to do if what Don John says is true? What is your opinion of Claudio and Don Pedro's reaction? What was said earlier in the play to prepare the reader for this reaction of Claudio?

ACT III, Scene 3

6.   What is the job of the watch? What does Dogberry tell the guards to do if they have trouble? What do the members of the watch conclude?

7.   How are Claudio and Don Pedro so easily fooled in the garden?

ACT III, Scene 4

8.   Why does Hero ask Margaret if she is not ashamed of what she had said? What is Margaret's response?

9.   As Hero prepares to leave for the church at the end of this scene, what surprise awaits her?

ACT III, Scene 5

10. Why does Leonato become impatient with Dogberry and Verges?

11. Explain what a malapropism is. Illustrate your definition with the following: decerns, odorous, excommunication. When Leonato says, "Neighbors, you are tedious," how does Dogberry take this comment?

ACT IV, Scene 1

1. After making a number of short comments, Claudio finally gets to his point. What does he say about the appearance of Hero and the reality of Hero?

2. Once Leonato understands what Claudio means, what does he initially suppose caused Claudio to condemn Hero? When Leonato turns to the prince for help, what is the prince's response?

3. Claudio tells us that he shall "lock up all the gates of love." Why will he do this?

4. Once Leonato believes Hero's accusation, what is his reaction after she faints? What is the friar's opinion, and what is his suggestion?

5. What is Benedick's reaction to Hero's accusation, and what is Beatrice's reaction? How does Beatrice get Benedick to agree to be her instrument of revenge?

6. Describe Leonato's reaction to Claudio's charge in this scene.

   At first,

   Then -

   But then -

ACT IV, Scene 2

7. How does Dogberry's limited knowledge of language add to the humor in this scene?

8. In the examination of the witnesses, what does Dogberry feel is most important? What is it about Dogberry that makes him a typical comic figure in a Shakespearean comedy?

ACT V, Scene 1

1. Describe what happens between Leonato, Antonio, Claudio and Don Pedro.

2. How do Don Pedro and Claudio first react to Benedick's challenge? What does Don Pedro mean when he says, "What a pretty thing man is when he goes in his doublet and hose and leaves off his wit!"

3. How does Don Pedro mock Dogberry?

4. Why does Borachio so readily confess his villainy? What is Don Pedro and Claudio's first reaction to this news?

5. What personal insult by Borachio does Dogberry insist be noted? What makes his insistence on this point so comical and ironic?

6. When Borachio says that he alone killed Hero, what is Leonato's sarcastic response?

7. For Claudio to make amends, what does Leonato require of Claudio? How guilty is Margaret in the conspiracy? In your opinion, how guilty is Claudio when he says the following?
   "…. Yet sinned I not
   But in mistaking."

ACT V, Scene 2

8. When Benedick says he was not born under a rhyming planet, of what is he complaining?

9. What is Beatrice's greatest concern when she meets Benedick? What is Benedick's response? What news does Ursula bring?

ACT V, Scene 4

10. What is the number one question to be answered in order to resolve all misunderstandings before this scen and the play?

11. At the wedding scene, why does Claudio not immediately recognize Hero? How does this masking of Hero, and ultimate unmasking of Hero, fit in with the play's major theme?

12. What resolution awaits Beatrice and Benedick?

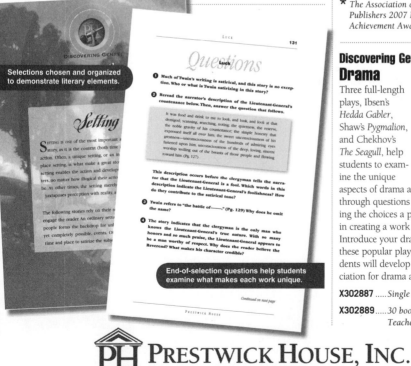